# ENDORSEM

D1120458

Contrary to what society tell us, real beauty is found on the inside first. Through the pages of **RISE.** you will see beauty rising from ashes. As former Miss Ohio USA, and Mrs. International, and author of **MISS CONCEPTION** it is refreshing to see someone as genuine and willing to be exposed as Debra. You can follow her journey through her misconceptions to her crowning moment. This book is a must read!

Lisa Moser
www.LisaMoser.com
www.MrsInternational.com


A great project with an incredible purpose behind it.

Dr. Ben Lerner
www.drbenlerner.com


When Debra first told me her story I felt in the depth of my soul that it was going to touch soooo many women and men. There are numerous people out there who NEED this open honest diary of her life co-mingled with her humor that those of us who know Debra LOVE. Working with post abortive women has opened my eyes to the value and healing **RISE** offers.

Angela Dee, author of **VOICELESS, SPENCER'S STORY**
www.angeladee.life


As relationship coaches and authors of **Help, I'm Stuck! Mistakes Christian Women Make When Pursuing Their Purpose** we encourage women to seek their relationship with God first. In the book, **RISE,** Debra takes you on her journey of discovering God is FOR her and not AGAINST her. Regardless of any mistakes, God has a beautiful plan for your life. Debra exposes her struggles, doubts and fears as a platform for others to relate. Her passion in *RISE* is for others to find their own abundant life on earth while knowing if they have children living in heaven that through Jesus they can hold that child again.

Dexter and Tiffany Godfrey
www.RelationshipMissionaries.com

The unfortunate reality is that at some point in our journey most of us will face the unwanted, unexpected challenges life can throw at us. Debra's personal journey is one that's had its share of those challenges. Her faith and endurance gives us practical, everyday encouragement, reminding us that we truly never fail if we refuse to quit. So, don't!! Debra's personal stories in *Rise* will encourage and motivate you. So, when it seems like hell won't back off, God will meet you right in the middle of your storm, giving you the strength to keep moving forward.

Gary Toney, Pastor, Victory Life Church
www.victorylifeonline.org

Overcoming obstacles begins with the right attitude. In *RISE*, you will be moved and entertained as you follow Debra's determined attitude to rise above the many devastating events she faced. I was Debra's producer on television and saw first- hand how she navigates obstacles. She always had an incredible ability to re-adjust and see things differently when problems occurred. Debra could have easily been a basket case at times but she always knew how to pull herself together to get the job done! Her "*the show must go on*" attitude was displayed not only in her work ethic but in her personal life. Her ability to see humor in situations is weaved throughout her personal stories in *RISE*. This book will encourage you to look above your own circumstances and find the strength to move forward.

Chris Reddick Producer/Director
www. VentureProductions.TV

The compassion and encouragement you will find in **RISE** are true expressions from the heart of a dear friend of mine. Debra was by our side after the tragic loss of my son-in-law. In this book, you will experience her passion to see people RISE above heartache and pain.

Debra helped me as a mother and grandmother to show my daughter and precious grandchildren how to hold on to God's promise that would carry us when we didn't know how to face the next day. She encouraged myself and my husband to discover the strength to help our family in supporting and guiding our little ones. She guided us in showing them that God didn't punish them and their daddy didn't do anything wrong. God healed their daddy in Heaven and someday they would see him again.

With Debra's love, compassion, and support through this tragic time we grew with the Lord. My grandchildren did not become victims instead they became followers of Christ. Two out of three have accepted the Lord at the age of 6. The other one is only 5 but, loves the Lord with her little heart. As a family, we take each day knowing that whatever we face, the Lord is going before us. Debra taught us to get back up and RISE to the next chapter. Our story wasn't over. Every day a new.

Shirley Devers Wife, Mother, Grandmother, Friend

# RISE

To Virginia
always RISE.

*Debra Lynn Hayes*

# RISE

## WHAT TO DO
## WHEN HELL WON'T
## BACK OFF

DEBRA LYNN HAYES

Copyright 2017 © by Debra Lynn Hayes

All Rights Reserved
Printed in the United States of America 2017 First Edition

Published by Author Academy Elite
P.O. Box 43 Powell, OH 43035
www.AuthorAcademyElite.com

All rights reserved. No part of this publication may be reproduced, stored in a retrieval system, or transmitted in any form or by any means – for example, electronic, photocopy, recording – without prior written permission of the publisher. The only exception is brief quotations in printed reviews.

Unless noted, all Bible quotations are from The Message Copyright ©2000 by Eugene H Peterson, NavPress Publishing Group PO Box 35001, Colorado Springs, CO 80935 Used by Permission

Scripture quotations marked NASB are taken from the New American Standard Bible*, Copyright © 1960, 1962, 1963, 1968, 1971, 1972, 1973, 1975, 1977, 1995 by The Lockman Foundation

Scripture quotations marked NIV are taken from the Holy Bible, New International Version*, NIV*, Copyright © 1973, 1978, 1984, 2011, by Biblica, Inc. ™ All rights reserved worldwide. www.zondervan.com The "NIV" and "New International Version" are trademarks registered in the United States Patent and Trademark Office by Biblica, Inc.™

Scripture quotations marked TLB are taken from The Living Bible copyright © 1971. Used by permission of Tyndale House Publishers, Inc. Wheaton, Illinois 60189 All rights reserved.

Scripture quotations marked AMP are taken from The Amplified* Bible, copyright © 1954, 1958, 1962, 1964, 1965, 1987, by The Lockman Foundation. Used by Permission (www.Lockman.com)

Scripture quotations marked NKJV are taken from New King James Version* ©1982 Thomas Nelson All rights reserved.

Photo Credits, Back Cover: Photo, Dr. Gregg Perry Makeup, Madison Shepard

Paperback ISBN:  978-1-946114-31-0
Hardback ISBN:  978-1-946114-32-7
LCCN:       2016921475

*For my four sons living in heaven*

**R** *– Randall*
**I** *– Isaac*
**S** *– Stefan*
**E** *– Ephraim*

*Knowing my story will be complete the day*
*I see and hold you again*

# CONTENTS

PART ONE
KNOCKED DOWN

# PART THREE
## SITTING

# PART FOUR
## RISE

# AUTHOR'S NOTE

*"And I feel like I'm naked in front of the crowd*
*Cause these words are my diary, screaming out loud*
*And I know that you'll use them however you want to"[1]*

I have chosen to expose my life and by doing so it automatically trickles into the lives of others. Some names have been omitted on purpose. This book is a snapshot of time. Life is a journey and people make choices to improve as they travel through. The lessons learned and taught through this book are more important than the names attached to the actions.

There is no desire to turn mistakes into documented landmarks. We are all like icebergs. What is seen on the surface rarely exposes what is underneath. Oftentimes what is underneath is unresolved pain. Everyone mentioned in the book has been given the grace to grow and move forward.

# FOREWORD

When I met Debra, she was, in her own words, "Stuck." She had survived some of the worst tragedies imaginable yet knew her life could mean more.

She was passionate to write a book in which she utilized her losses and mistakes to help others. She chose the hard road and revisited every wound for additional healing and clarity before she wrote the first word.

While working through *The Deeper Path* and *Your Secret Name,* both courses of intense transformation, I saw her come alive in a new way.

When she brought me her subtitle, "What To Do When Hell Won't Back Off", as her coach, my initial thoughts were that it was a little too strong. The more I learned of her life, the more I realized what a good fit it was. The strength of her subtitle matches the strength it took Debra to navigate the pain she endured.

***RISE*** will not only encourage a deeper relationship with your Creator, it is also the perfect gift for a struggling friend. Debra's depth, simplicity, and often humorous views of life make it a thought-provoking read.

Kary Oberbrunner
CEO of Redeem the Day and Igniting Souls.
Co-creator of Author Academy Elite.
Author of *Day Job to Dream Job, The Deeper Path,* and
*Your Secret Name* and *ELIXIR Project*

# INTRODUCTION
## WHAC A MOLE MOURNINGS

I am drawing this name from a game I played with my son. Living in Ohio, we were within minutes of Kings Island Amusement Park. Whac a Mole™¹ was located inside the busy carnival section and consisted of a board with five cut out holes. The plastic moles would pop their heads through the holes one at a time. The goal was to take your mallet and quickly beat the mole's head back down each time he raised it. As time went on, the game became faster and more challenging. Looking back over the 1990's (which I refer to as the decade from Hell) those years resembled this game. I was the mole. Not only did it feel like I was in a dark box trying to find the light, but each time I raised my head I was forcefully knocked back down.

Have you ever looked at life and wondered how in the world it ended up like it did? As I look in the mirror this question is constantly in the forefront of my mind. A little girls' dreams of being a loving wife and mother in a house full of children, pets, and constant chaos were shattered by bad decisions and the tragic deaths of three children. The pieces of my life did not come together as I had dreamed. From the lost visions of holding cooing babies, I found myself in an international corporate business position. I spent several years traveling and enjoying this world God created. I had the pleasure of experiencing our beautiful country in ways most people only see in photographs.

I hosted a TV show in my hometown after my travels ended. Woven into the amazingly pleasant times of my life was a continuous thread of loss. At age fifteen I lost a friend who was as close to me as any brother would be. Because of that broken heart, I went through three broken engagements. I let circumstances and fear take the best of my reasoning which resulted in an abortion. As a daddy's girl, I watched cancer claim my father. I gave birth to a precious little boy that was stillborn. Thirteen short months later I was in the same maternity ward giving birth to a second baby boy who only lived an hour. Three years later my nineteen- year old step-son, whom I adored, was killed in an accident. As the spiral of losses continued I lost my marriage, a house, and landed in financial ruin.

While I tell my story, I am not in any way seeking pity, nor do I think for one minute that my losses are worse than the pain and hurts other people experience. The intention of this book is to connect with anyone facing their own dark days and offer some rays of hope. I do not claim to have done everything right in the healing process. I went from blaming God and being angry at Him to carrying all the condemnation and guilt of my bad decisions on my shoulders. I was convinced that God had punished me for that abortion with the death of my three sons. My own forgiveness was the hardest to accept. After learning to love myself, I saw God as a loving father and my best friend not the thief I had perceived.

I do not claim to have always had the most loving and appropriate attitude toward God nor people. All I can offer is a view into my bad decisions, my hurts, and my pain and the encouragement that anyone can survive. I do not intend to preach or evangelize, only to share lessons I have learned. I will share the Scriptures that helped me the most. They are direct Scriptures which were answers to raw emotions. I encourage any hurting person reading this to search out Scriptures for themselves. (I will help you with that in Part Four). God has a way of taking even one sentence and giving life and hope.

It would be nice to say that I quietly and meekly submitted to Scriptures with inner strength and sweet little prayers of survival. Nothing could be further from the truth. I will say that God was and is my rock, but wow, did we ever go through some battles to get to a place of acceptance and peace. Honestly, sometimes certain circumstances will trigger those battles again. Life is a journey that goes from *I think I've got this!* to *Where did these emotions and tears come from again so quickly?* An important part of overcoming tragedies and deep hurt is realizing that it's an "ING" thing. I had to keep goING, hopING, seekING, reachING, oftentimes cryING, screamING, and occasionally even cussING. The most important thing for me was to be real with myself and with God about where I was emotionally. He was neither shocked nor surprised when I became totally transparent. In fact, He already knew. He did not fall off His throne when I approached him boldly and honestly. I will share vivid examples of this in future chapters.

Some people say, "Time cures all wounds." I do not believe this. Time can move us away from the point of pain. However, if we choose to run from the pain instead of toward it, the future decisions we make can be greatly affected. The unresolved pain can create a paralyzing shield around our hearts.

Each of my losses were completely different. One would think that losing two infants thirteen months apart would bring the same emotions, questions and experience. Not at all, they were totally different. My prayer is, as I expose my life, it may touch a place where someone has stopped in the healing process or given up. Each day is a new day. His mercies are indeed new every morning. Lamentations 3:22-23 NASB "The Lord's loving kindness indeed never ceases. For his compassions never fail. They are new every morning. Great is Thy faithfulness." I have often rephrased that to say His Mercies are New Every MOURNING.

# PART ONE
## KNOCKED DOWN

*"Wage it alone and start to come undone"*

Collin Raye, *"Undefeated"*

# 1

## A BEAUTIFUL BEGINNING—
## A THREAD OF LONELINESS

I grew up in a loving home as an only child. My parents were everything any child could want. We were not the wealthiest in town, we didn't live in the grandest house, but our home was full of love. My father was a pleasant, hardworking, and humorous man. I never heard an unkind word come from his mouth nor an unkind tone in his voice. My Mom was filled with unconditional love. She always thought of others before she thought of herself. How could any child feel like anything was missing from their life?

Loneliness was my constant companion. Having the personality that loves people and socialization, I always felt the void of not having siblings. I did find ways to entertain myself. I often lived in a vicarious world of baby dolls and Barbie dolls. Outdoor adventures of my unique design brought their own excitement. There was a large boathouse in our back yard. It had a dirt floor and four open sides. A wooden shelf was located half way up on three of the four sides. That made a perfect rack for baking my mud pies in the sun. A small sidewalk trailed along the side of the yard. Even as a small girl I remember taking my tricycle to the top of the slightly inclined sidewalk and letting myself go in the wind. With legs extended straight out and pedals rotating faster than the blades of a fan set on high, there was no chance of putting my feet down to stop. I sped down the asphalt only to come to an abrupt halt in the grass.

Mom had a sweet way of interrupting my adventurous after-noons by bringing out a colored cake she baked. She would use food coloring to make the simplest cakes fun. Green was my favorite. She would always make an extra one for the little boy living next door who was mentally challenged. It was most likely her way of making up for the days I tried to convince him that my mud pies were to die for.

School offered some relief from loneliness. Kindergarten was okay. What I remember the most were the crafts I was not very good at and the naps. Really? Naps were necessary when we were only there half a day? First grade was better. My teacher was a friend of our family and I looked forward to attending her class. She gave me my first fifteen minutes of fame.

One Sunday afternoon my parents and I had visited her family farm. I was so excited to interact with the animals. My mistake was thinking the animals were just as excited to see me. I got a little too close to the pony from behind. He kicked and his huff landed with a solid hit across my foot. The story sounded a little more dramatic as she told it in class on Monday. That little story and the small amount of attention it brought to me seemed to open doors to make friends and playmates.

School was fun but it made coming home in the afternoon that much lonelier. Instead of being outside, I found myself spending more time in front of the TV. Instead of baby dolls and Barbie dolls, I now lived my life vicariously through *The Brady Bunch* and *The Partridge Family*. I would watch these shows over and over secretly pretending that I was one of the characters. My dream to live in a house full of brothers, sisters, pets and constant chaos was portrayed on those shows.

I can't remember a time in my life when I didn't love music. At age six the top of my birthday cake had mini figures of *The Beatles*. During later elementary school years and early junior high school I would go to sleep with the timer on the radio set to a favorite Knoxville station. "American Pie"[1] lullabied me to sleep many nights.

I was seven when Mom enrolled me in piano lessons. Naturally, there were classic beginner pieces a student must learn to play. I was very compliant and eager to learn everything I could. However, when it came time for my first recital the teacher and I did not see eye to eye. Her idea of a nice recital piece was "The Flight of the Bumblebee."[2] My idea of performing at the piano was "Wichita Lineman"[3] by Glen Campbell. I had become a big fan while watching *The Glen Campbell Goodtime Hour*. I don't remember what persuasion I used to get my way, but boldly in the recital program beside "The Flight of the Bumblebee"[4] and "Fur Elise"[5] (done by other students) was "Wichita Lineman"[6] by Debbie Hayes. No doubt it lost its pizzazz when performed by a beginner piano student.

I pursued playing the flute in the school band beginning in the 5th grade. During my 6th grade year I was chosen as the drum major for the all city elementary school band. Even though I had a good understanding of music, I am certain, it was because I had grown several inches taller than my classmates. Everyone could see me marching in front of the band. Junior high school brought on one of my first trips without my parents. The junior high band was going to Banner Elk, NC for a week of band camp.

Band camp was hot with a lot of marching. I had not calculated into my "fun" trip away that most of the down time would be spent memorizing music on my flute. I quickly noticed a sign announcing the date and times for drum major tryouts. I wasn't aware they had tryouts because I had been "picked" by the director in elementary school. I started thinking: *What do I have to lose? If I didn't make it, I wouldn't be any worse off. If I did make it, I would not have to continue memorizing that music.* The only other way to get out of memorizing the music was to be a majorette but I could not twirl a baton. So off to drum major try outs I went.

As expected, a lot of the tryouts involved directing music, at which I was confident with. Making drum major of the junior high school band came as a surprise and a relief. To this day, I do feel a little guilty that I came into tryouts at the last minute and won when several girls had prepared and dreamed of getting that position. But after all, if you never *just go for it* the opportunity can pass. Don't ever ignore that nudging inside. That quiet little voice inside is often leading you in the perfect direction. If you hesitate, or over think the situation, you could miss some awesome opportunities in your life. Granted, I had not gone to band camp with the intention of trying out for drum major yet my experience had prepared me for the moment.

Marching in our hometown parades presented one fear no other junior high or even high school band in the country was faced with. Not only was our Main Street lined with sidewalks, we had a Sky Walk. At the printing of this book, Morristown, Tennessee remained the only town in the United States with overhead sidewalks. While marching west to east through the middle of downtown, we could see shoulder to shoulder people crowded beside us and above us. An overhead sidewalk stretched across the street at every block. I was beginning to have second thoughts about my *well thought out* drum major position as I passed underneath the overhead sidewalks. Was someone standing on the Sky Walk just waiting to take aim and spit on me?? At least the band members who were willing to memorize their music were wearing hats.

That year the band went on to win a couple of field show competitions. My Dad became everyone's favorite person. After marching in those hot uniforms, he would have iced cold coca-colas waiting at the bus.

Daddy ran a little grocery store in our small town. It was unique during the 1970's because it was a quick stop market. There weren't convenient stores on every corner. It was the only place in town that stayed open past 9pm. He kept fresh seasonal fruits and vegetables along with all the normal staples for a kitchen. His personality was fun to be around, so people would gravitate there just to hang out. Most of his employees were young men who were in either high school or college. Over the years many of them have contacted me. Each telling the same story of how Daddy helped to mold their lives for the better.

As I moved toward my high school years I spent more time at that little store. I was never on the payroll, but Daddy always found things for me to do that was within my ability. For example, I learned to use the cash register and count money to customers without a calculator. He invested time developing my work ethic, people skills, and business sense. As with most small businesses, the workers became like family.

# 2

## THE BROTHER—
## I ALWAYS WANTED

This was without a doubt a challenging section of the book to write because it has almost been completely blocked from my memory. Yet it leaves the biggest impact on my life. While I was in junior high Daddy hired a young guy to work for him. Eddie was going to the University of Tennessee at the time to complete his master's degree. He was full of life and constantly joking around. I am not exactly sure when it began, but Eddie took the role of an older brother with me. He already had an older sister and a younger sister so I guess in his mind I became the baby sister. As I wrote about this time of my life I could only draw from snapshots of my time with him.

I remember he would interfere in my activities because he was so protective. I was going white water rafting on a river that was only a class one and two. The day was planned until Eddie got wind of the trip. He made a beeline for my mom with a convincing argument of how dangerous that would be for me. He won!!

As I mentioned earlier, the small group of employees were like family. On Sunday evenings after church Mom and I would always stop by the store to see Daddy. One Sunday evening, I was being a typical preteen "starving" for a pizza. Neither Mom nor Daddy were in the mood for pizza. Eddie said, "Where's your keys? I'll take her." There was a local pizzeria one block away so it was a win –win for us all. I got my pizza and Eddie took me while on the clock. Can't beat that! That became a weekly Sunday night event. Of course, every week I got to tell him all about the transition from junior high to high school, all about my boy crushes and the subjects I loved and hated. He never failed to have brotherly advice for me.

Eddie drove a little Volkswagon beetle. I loved to go for our Sunday night brother/sister dinners in this car. One Sunday, after we ate, he pulled into an empty parking lot. He looked at me and said, "Are you ready to learn to drive?" Well, yeah, I was 13 after all! We proceeded to change seats and the driving lessons began! The car had a manual transmission, so you can only imagine the hopping that beetle did. Eddie was a ton of fun but also a very determined individual. He would not let me fail. This became our Sunday night secret. I was driving, if only around empty parking lots. I finally had my older brother.

You had to drive up a small incline to get into the parking lot of our favorite fast food restaurant. Up until that time I had gotten the hang of the clutch and changing gears on flat asphalt. But that Sunday evening, it was time to do hills. Fortunately, there were no other cars close by. I can remember laughing uncontrollably each time I let the car roll backwards and die. Eddie would get frustrated but would not let me quit until I had it.

Unknowingly, those secret driving lessons were planting seeds inside me to never quit, never give up, and to get back up each time I got knocked down.

# 3
## BROTHER #2—
## I NOTICED A MOTORCYCLE

The store was small with a gravel parking lot on the side. One day as Mom and I drove into the parking lot I noticed a motorcycle parked next to the building. Inside was a new employee. Frank had been hired to share the same shifts with Eddie. He was also attending the University of Tennessee while majoring in physical education. It didn't take long for their friendship to take root.

I'm not convinced Frank would have been so eager to adopt me as a little sister without Eddie's influence. They began playing tennis together on their days off. Not wanting to be left out, I became the tag along sister. I didn't have a racket so Frank provided one from his collection of old rackets. That was the funniest racket I had ever seen. It was an old wooden racket. The head was so warped you could hold it up in front of your face and almost see through both sides, but that was fine. I had two brothers and a tennis racket. They didn't make much progress with me on the court, but I was perfectly content just hanging out to watch them play.

Holidays were fun times at the little store. Each season brought its own line of novelty items to sell. The storefront was open and filled with whatever fresh fruit or vegetable was in season. There were two short walkways leading to the doors. Between those walkways sat a large basket of raw peanuts inviting any customer to take a handful as they entered or exited. Above the entrance hung a small revolving light with red, green, and yellow bulbs. During the Easter season, yellow, pink and purple inflatable bunnies hung across the front blowing in the wind. On one side was a rather large cage with a few live rabbits to sell.

Eddie was constantly talking, singing, or whistling while he was outside working. We would notice that when he would go by the rabbit cage whistling, a little black and white Dutch rabbit would always lift its head, stop, and raise up on its back paws. We named him "Whistles". I adored that little rabbit. Eddie bought Whistles for me and built him his own cage. Mom wouldn't let me take Whistles home, so the guys kept him at the store and we all pitched in to care for him. Whistles remained with us for quite a while.

At the same time, Eddie adopted one of the rabbits for himself. "Slick" was brown and much larger than Whistles. Eddie was not content to keep him in a cage. No, Slick must be trained. Before long that rabbit was hopping around following Eddie's every move. As you came inside the store there was a waist high counter where the local daily newspapers were stacked. Slick was trained to sit alone on the newspapers. One day after school I came in to check on my Whistles and found Eddie and Slick in the backroom with a towel and several large safety pins. The rabbit had peed all over the local newspapers. I joined in the feat of holding a wiggly, kicking rabbit while he was being diapered. Finally, the crazy fun chaotic times I had been dreaming of.

Often the simple things in life, that some people long for, are the very things other people take for granted.

The summer before I started high school I was asked on my first date. My parents had known the guy since he was born. He was a 12th grade senior and would stop by the store each day after football practice. I thought this date was the coolest thing ever. Me, a freshman, had been asked on a date by a senior. Not to mention, he had the neatest little two-seater red convertible sports car. As I was telling Eddie about it, his face went from smiling to frowning. He made a beeline for Mom. In his opinion, I was indeed too young to date. The senior football player was too old for me. Who was going to go with us? Where did he plan to take me? What time did he need to have me home? He had to keep me in Morristown, we could NOT go to Knoxville. I could not wear shorts or a short skirt. I should cancel it and wait another year before I started dating. This was the side of an older brother I wasn't very excited about. Daddy and Mama did let me go with restrictions, but I don't think Eddie spoke to them for a while.

I know these little stories seem silly and juvenile, but words cannot adequately describe the fulfillment Eddie and Frank brought to my life.

# 4

# WAS UNLIKE HIM TO BE LATE— THEN THE PHONE CALL CAME

The time came for Eddie to be at work. It was totally unlike him to be late, but it was even rarer for there to be no communication from him. Then the phone call came. He had turned left onto the four-lane boulevard on his way to work, and had been broadsided by one of the drivers of two cars that had decided to race. Our little beetle was knocked several feet into the roadside embankment. I have no memory from the time I was told about the phone call until we were at the funeral home. I have been told he was rushed to Knoxville and had emergency surgery trying to save his life.

Walking in the funeral home was like walking into a silent movie. People were moving in slow motion. Mouths were moving, but I could hear nothing. I walked down the short hall into the chapel and glanced to my right. There he was. The distance between me and that casket seemed miles upon miles. I wanted to run out and find my brother and cry, but he was the one laying in that casket. I glanced to my left and saw Frank sitting on the sofa along the back wall. He stood up and extended his hand, and we made that long walk to the casket together.

Everything inside me shut down at that very moment. I have no memory of the funeral. I have no memory of going to the graveyard. Even though I have been to his grave to take flowers several times throughout the years, still nothing about being there jogs any memories. The only memory I have other than the funeral home is someone telling me that when they went through his wallet he had three pictures in it. There was one of his older sister. There was one of his younger sister. There was one of me.

Frank and I became closer after going through this tragedy. Shortly after Eddie died Frank gave up any birthday plans he could have made that year to help my best friend Beth and I roll (or TP) yards. Love his heart, we loaded his car with toilet paper (donated by Daddy of course) and had the route mapped for the houses we wanted to hit. He would patiently sit in his car waiting for us to finish one shenanigan after another then say, "Where to now"?

Many hours were also spent coaching me on the tennis court...... with a brand-new racket. Competitive tennis most likely would not have interested me, yet Frank signed me up for my first tournament without my knowledge. From that, it became a passion. He has indeed been a brother figure to me over the years and remains so to this day.

At the time of Eddie's passing my shock and memory blocks served me well. Even as I have written this I have allowed myself to have feelings and shed tears that have not been there since that dreadful time.

Does the Bible really say God will not allow us to be given more than we can handle? Correct me if I am wrong, but I have never found that in there. The verse that is often misquoted is not talking about pain at all. It is making a reference to temptation. It is 1 Corinthians 10:13 NASB "No temptation has overtaken you but such as is common to man, and God is faithful, who will not allow you to be tempted beyond what you are able, but with temptation will provide the way of escape also, that you may be able to endure it" The Message paraphrase says it this way. "No test or temptation that comes your way is beyond the course of what others have had to face. All you need to remember is that God will never let you down, he'll never let you be pushed past your limit: he'll always be there to help you come through it" These verses are making a reference to situations where you find yourself having a chance to make a right decision or be tempted in another direction.

What happens when the situation has nothing to do with choice? What about the circumstances, like death, that you have no control over? What about the pain that goes so deep it numbs your heart? Yes indeed, I believe some pain is more than we can handle. These are the times when only the grace of God keeps those mountains of pain from crushing us. At those times, we can choose to cling to God the best way we can or begin to mask the pain in various ways or both. Sometimes the masking is harmful and self-destructive such as excesses in substances or sex. Other times it is simply hedges we build around our heart.

How does a fifteen- year- old process the pain of losing someone so close? Well…I didn't. That pain remained inside and has shown itself in many ways throughout my life. That was the loss that I remembered the least, yet the one that impacted my life the most. Looking back, I can see a pattern that developed from losing Eddie. The people I cared for the most in my life, I would only let so close then I would push them away for fear of losing them. It happened numerous times with the men I would date. When it would not hurt very much to lose someone, my heart was wide open to them. But once I began to feel true love for someone, rather than embrace them, I would find a way to run. Often by creating distance or leaving them hanging without any answers. I was attempting desperately to protect my heart from being hurt again.

"But given enough time, Pain eventually breaks through and corners us. When it does, most of us run for cover. We numb ourselves, because when we're numb we don't feel anything – the good or the bad. We shout for our savior, noise, to come rescue us and drown out our ache. We busy ourselves by asking activity to join us"[1]

# 5

## COLLEGE—
## LET'S GO TO PLAN B

My senior year was my least favorite of the twelve years of school. I had been involved with a close group of friends from my church since my freshman year. Most were older, so throughout my four years of high school they were continually graduating. The guys I dated were also older and I had seen them graduate and go off to college as well. I tried to make a long- distance relationship work with a couple of them but we were too young and college was a much different lifestyle than high school. After losing Eddie, each time a close friend graduated and moved on it tugged at a deep place in my heart.

I had applied to several colleges and was accepted by all. My choice was a small private Baptist college about fifteen miles from my home town. That choice resulted more from it being the more acceptable place to go than any research or deep thought about my future. My best friend Beth was going there, and after all, we had done life together since second grade. Several of my church group friends were already there, so why not? I had all the paperwork done and a roommate had been assigned.

Graduation night from High School was a hoot. What was meant to be a small party with a few close girlfriends had turned into the city- wide graduation event. We had two high schools in our little town. One on the east side of town and one on the west. At the time, however, there was only one junior high school. My classmates and I were in classes together for two years during the seventh and eighth grade then we were divided between the two high schools for the ninth grade through twelfth. One street going north and south through town was the deciding mark. It made the competition interesting between the two high schools because the students were friends as well as new rivals.

Graduation was held on the same day for both schools. By early evening, all had gone through pomp and circumstance. My aunt Marie was visiting from St. Louis and wanted to do something special for the occasion. We had planned to have a few girlfriends over for a nice quiet get together. The word started spreading. How could I say no to other girlfriends who wanted to come? Before long the guys were asking to come as well. Why not? Then a classmate told me that our friends at West High were also planning to come. At that point, the answer became: Everyone is welcome but no alcohol per Mom's request. That party was coming together. And it did...... in a big way!

Our house was full. Our patio was full. Our yard was full. A good friend was the DJ at a dance across town. Just past midnight he showed up at my house with the disco machine and cranked it up full blast in the back yard. Daddy had gone to graduation but he was back at the store for the final hours before closing that night.

The police got a couple of phone calls from neighbors about the noise. Since the store was the usual hang out for the deputies, they knew about the party. Their response was to simply drive through the neighborhood then go back to the store with the remarks, "At least we know where most of the graduates in this town are tonight. We are not interrupting that." Response was only passed through a phone call to Mom to watch the noise. All my friends respected the "no alcohol at the party" request, however, there were several thirsty trips secretly made to cars that night. Graduation night turned out to be one of my favorite memories of my senior year.

The summer between high school and college brought the first of several financial changes for our family. Daddy did not own the store. He ran it and split the profits 50/50 with the owner. It had been successful enough that two families lived very comfortably.

However, without discussion, the owner decided to sell and Daddy was left with nothing to go to and nothing to fall back on. He was very well known in the town for his work ethic and personality so he was immediately hired by a larger grocery store in the town. It did not provide the same atmosphere nor the same income. Yet, he never complained about anything. He took it all in stride and gave every day one hundred percent.

It became obvious that a private college was becoming a big concern. Yet, that concern was never expressed to me. My parents would have sacrificed whatever it took to fulfill my dreams. The biggest dream at that time was to be a fitness instructor, play tennis, have fun and find a way to get paid for it. I was sensitive for the financial direction our family was going and was feeling guilt and compassion for Daddy trying to find a way to make my college work.

Walters State Community College had been built in our town a few years before I graduated. It was a two-year college that offered the basic classes any freshmen or sophomore needed for a fraction of the price. That only made sense to me. If I attended there, it would take the pressure off my parents for a couple of years. Since many students stayed in town and attended, it seemed like high school all over again in another building. In fact, we had nicknamed it Wally High. The only problem was it was a little too familiar and conveniently located next door to the Racquet Club where Frank was the tennis Pro and I was employed part time. Amazingly, during snowfalls I could not drive to classes but spent the entire day at the Racquet Club. I accomplished my goals of playing tennis, having fun and finding a way to get paid. However, it took me nowhere. After two years, I pursued a job selling insurance. The people skills and work ethics instilled in me by Daddy provided much success over the years. Eventually I ended up in a position as a corporate liaison for an international company. Even though I was blessed to achieve levels of success without a degree, I do regret not being focused and not completing college.

# 6

## BROKEN ENGAGEMENTS—
## TAKE IT ON THE RUN

When it came to heart issues I would make one wrong decision after another. I let a couple of amazing high school sweethearts slip by because I pushed them away. It had only been a few years since Eddie had passed and I still had a hedge of protection around my heart. Over time, this little heart game I was playing, resulted in three broken engagements. Two were great guys and one......well that was clearly God's protection over my life. In fact, when I took the man that I eventually did marry to a family gathering and introduced him as my fiancé, one of my aunts said, "Please don't think we are rude if we don't act too excited We have been this far a few times before." Seriously? I am sure THAT made him feel special.

Engagement *NUMBER ONE* was a couple of years out of high school. The gentleman was a wonderful guy and treated me great. I loved him and his family and can't remember having any bad feelings toward him at all. We both realized we were young and things just didn't feel right to move forward. One of the biggest factors in things not feeling right was that hedge around my heart. We are friends to this day and keep in touch.

Engagement *NUMBER TWO* was like something out of a fairy tale. I was in my mid- twenties. Through some unusual circumstances, I met a guy who lived in a large metro city several hundred miles away. I was passing through Dallas to meet some mutual friends on my way to Colorado for a week of skiing. There was an immediate attraction. He was one of the best- looking men I had ever seen. He was a model. *Tall, dark, and handsome* could not begin to describe his appearance. It was a brief encounter as I passed through the city.

A few weeks after I had returned from skiing he contacted me through our mutual friends. It became a full year of one of the best long distance relationships anyone could imagine. We made several trips between Dallas and Tennessee getting to know each other as well as friends and families. Our friends referred to us as *Ken and Barbie.* What could be missing? He was an honest sincere Christian, was an absolute hunk, was successful in his vocation and he treated me like a queen.

A winter vacation the following year forced me to face my familiar fears. We had left a cozy fire in a ski lodge and walked outside to sit underneath the clear starry sky. The bright snowy slopes of the majestic Rocky Mountains made a perfect backdrop to begin talking about a long life together. My heart was barely beginning to peep over the hedge of protection and embrace a bright future. The more we talked the tighter my throat became and the faster my head began to spin.

"How did we make that move? Was I ready to leave a small town and move to a metro city? Do I want to leave my family and go to a place so far away? I couldn't drive home whenever I wanted to. I had never lived outside East Tennessee. What if I got there and something went wrong? What if I missed my parents too much?" Welcome to my world of living in fear. Compliments of the hedge around my heart!!!!!

As a transition, he offered to move me to Dallas initially without committing to marriage. Several of the girlfriends, I had gotten to know while visiting, offered to let me live with them until I was ready to make the BIG commitment. He was going to pay all my expenses during this transition so I could be comfortable and sure. What more could a girl dream of or ask for?

BUT WAIT! My heart was too vulnerable! I needed to protect it from future pain! I couldn't open my heart that much! RUN!!!!

Broken engagement #2!!!!!!! I don't know where this guy is today, but he was my one that got away. I pray God blessed him with a loving wife and family.

Engagement *NUMBER THREE* is certainly a tale to be told. All I can say is I thank God for his protection over my life. I had begun going to a church where there was a lot of emphasis put on marriage. Granted, marriage is God's beautiful example on this earth of his covenant love for his church. However, with so much importance put on marriage, I saw people begin "making" marriages happen in their lives instead of using common sense and letting God lead. I saw hearts crushed and lives ruined. At the same time, I saw examples of marriages worthy of taking note of.

A new guy had begun coming to the church. He was genuinely seeking God and looking to live a clean life after leaving a lifestyle of drugs and addictions. He was the owner of the fitness center where I worked out. I knew him and naturally we became better friends after he started attending the church. He asked me to attend a weekly Bible study, so each week we would travel an hour north to Johnson City, TN to that meeting. Our friendship grew into a very healthy relationship sincerely "seeking God" together. With the influence and the environment of the church, we began believing God was leading us down the road toward marriage. If simple common sense that God gave us had ruled, I would have known that anyone coming out of an addiction needs time. Yet I was too young for common sense and it sure seemed to be "God".

We started discussing plans for marriage. After all, I had run twice before so I needed to get my head together, trust God, and make a commitment. Things were moving quickly but smoothly. He was making all the legal arrangements for me to become half owner in the fitness center. (a dream come true...my goal of working out and getting paid for it.) He bought a house and we were doing all the furniture shopping together. I can honestly say it was a good thing but maybe not a "God" thing. We were content, peaceful, and happy. Because of his background, some of my friends were questioning my decision. My response was, "But don't we believe in a God who can transform lives?" Yes, of course we do, and yes, he certainly does. But marriage this quickly??

One afternoon I was cleaning his new house preparing for him to move in. He came in with a flushed look on his face. A girl he had previously dated had called giving him the news that she was five months pregnant with his child. Confusion overtook him. Do we follow what we had perceived to be "God" leading us, or does he turn and marry the mother of his child? We were advised to take a time of separation so he could think clearly. The dreams I had begun to dream were crushed with his decision to marry someone else. All the plans we were making together abruptly ended with that one phone call. Maybe I wasn't as heartbroken at losing him as I was confused. I had finally decided to break my pattern of running, but I still ended up, what I perceived to be, the loser. I was beginning to think that if I wasn't sabotaging and causing my own disappointment that God would intervene and sabotage it for me.

If it weren't enough to be doubting myself and God, the pastor of the church stepped in to make this confusion even greater. I only add this to say be very careful who you choose to have any authoritative input in your life. You should measure any advice against the Word of God not the word of a man. If it measures up, you are safe. If not, let it go!! I wish I had.

The Senior Pastor of the church wanted to discuss the situation that had just occurred. Thinking it was to offer some encouragement, I went to his office. The entire conversation revolved around "procreation". I was getting a sermonette on sex and he couldn't even say the word. "Procreation" was the word of choice. I was basically being accused of a sex centered relationship. Admittedly, I may not have been a pure white virgin up to that point, but in that relationship, we had purposely chosen not to have sex until we were married. We HAD NOT had sex during the time we were together. However, I guess it was easier to make the desired assumptions for the prepared sermonette than to seek the truth.

I encourage you, if anything similar has occurred in your life where you begin to do things the "right" way and it still backfires on you, KEEP GOING. Do not stop with a pity party about the fairness of life. Life's not fair, and while we are on this earth, people will not treat you fairly. God is just but earth time is not fair and sometimes it just simply sucks. God sees you and knows exactly where you are. If your heart is clear with him DO NOT let the position a man holds speak condemnation to you.

I began questioning myself by thinking I should feel bad and guilty like something I had done had brought this abrupt disappointment to my life. I couldn't exactly pinpoint what actions were wrong but if the "Gods' person" felt it was important enough to call me in, surely something was my fault. I knew it wasn't sex but I took that condemnation and carried it away with me anyway. That was a powerful interaction. (well there wasn't a lot of interaction, it was primarily him talking and me listening) But it began to paralyze my heart and distort my thoughts of myself and God.

Looking back many years later I could see that God had indeed intervened to stop that engagement. He didn't do it to cause me pain but had stopped it to protect my life from future pain and stress. He didn't cause any of the circumstances that occurred. Each one of us makes choices that we are forced to live with. However, I believe that man did seek God in his decision and God led him to marry the woman carrying his child.

As the years played out, that man was again caught in the trap of addiction and destructive actions to himself and others. His life ended in a scene of criminal drama. That engagement indeed proved to be a time when a small amount of heart-ache and tears outweighed the potential devastation down the road. However, I could not see that at the time.

There is a colloquialism called Blinding Pain. It focuses on physical pain but I believe that blinding pain is not always physical. Oftentimes, the emotional pain we choose to hold onto causes us to see things differently than they are and make wrong choices for our lives.

One of my favorite quotes is from a French born American Author Anais Nin. He wrote, "We don't see things the way they are, we see things the way we are."

Emotional blinding pain almost always stems from a lie we have chosen to believe. That lie originates from our enemy Satan himself. Sometimes it is a wrong thought we hold to or as the story above shows, we allow someone else's words to plant that lie. When those lies take root, it is natural to gravitate toward a comfortable place, situation, or relationship to ease the pain or sometimes avoid the pain altogether. If we don't hit the pain and lies head on to let God do the work bringing truth, the pain will continually cycle back around. It's no secret that we have an enemy who would love to see us in that cycle. (John 10:10 The thief comes only to steal and kill and destroy. I came that they might have life and have it more abundantly).

The pain and obstacles thrown at our lives will indeed keep us on that merry-go -round of bad choices or seemingly comfortable places. Ironically those comfortable places never end up being that comfortable because inside we know there is more. It usually requires us making an uncomfortable and often drastic choice to discover the complete healing and the abundance on the other side. The abundant life in John 10:10 is not be speaking of material things as much as a full heart.

Genesis 50:20 also addresses the hurts and pains in our lives that can keep us on that merry-go-round. (...you planned evil against me but God used those same plans for my good...) We have an enemy. Life sucks sometimes and it can be cruel. Be willing to take those steps into the unknown and uncertain circumstances toward the fulfillment you are seeking. God is faithful to meet you right in the middle of your pain. He can take everything in your life that was meant to harm you and use it for good. Take a chance! God is not only the author but he is the finisher!!! Do that uncomfortable thing that God is leading you to do and find fulfillment!!!!!!

# 7

## BIGGEST MISTAKE—
## OF MY LIFE

The small town I grew up in eventually became too small. I had moved to Athens, TN for work. Not that Athens was any larger, but it offered some space to refocus from the fiasco I had been through. I had become close friends with a couple that had moved there from Atlanta. We shared mutual friends from my hometown. I still carried the false guilt and condemnation I had let the last "God's person" attach to my thoughts. I was walking in a cloud of guilt for something I had not even done. If it had not been for this couple who sincerely loved the Lord, I probably would have never walked back into a church. But I agreed to go with them Sunday after Sunday. Secretly, I was hoping to find a place that offered hope instead of condemnation. Only one seemed to offer what we were looking for. We had been attending several months and acquired many friends. The pastor and his family lived two houses away from me. I had gotten to know them well because it was a time in the South when neighbors would sit and chat on their porches.

I lived in a large structure that housed four townhomes. The parking was behind the building and it could only be accessed by driving down a narrow alleyway. One evening I was in my living room and heard a knock on the back door. It was the pastor of the church. Innocently, I let him in. He came in the living room where I was working on a project and proceeded to have meaningless conversation. Within an hour, he had invited me to go away with him to a golf resort for the weekend. He made no physical advances, just an invitation to spend the weekend together. WHAT??? ARE YOU SERIOUS?? SHUT THE BACK DOOR!!!

I obviously said no and asked him to leave. I became angry rather than confused at that, so I made a call to my friends from Atlanta. The next day they called him, but he did not return the call. After many attempts, they made a call to the elders of the church. Long story short, it was discovered that this was not the first time. It was a lifestyle for him. That was another disappointment in someone who should have been trustworthy. Life was beginning to add yet another layer of distrust in anyone who represented themselves as "God's person."

Again, I only add these stories about disappointment in pastors because I know there are many people in this world who have been wounded by a "God's person." I am sure many people have been hurt worse than I. My wounds were only verbal. However, the scars go deep because I was expecting so much more from someone in that position. Someone else could have said the very same things and it would not have left the same impact. When it comes to pastors or any spiritual authority in our lives I believe we can take a lesson from Jesus in John 2. He had attended the Passover Feast and discovered the leaders of the Temple had turned it into a marketplace for selling cattle, sheep, and doves as well as corruptly exchanging foreign money. He made a whip from ropes and chased both people and livestock out of the Temple. He scattered the money changers coins all over the floor and turned over the tables.

I am not suggesting anyone destroy a building because someone proves to be untrustworthy. But I do suggest to you that people in leadership are just people and oftentimes throughout history have disappointed, taken advantage of, and hurt other people. And when they do make mistakes the Bible is clear about restoration for that person. However, people are still damaged in the process. If you have ever been extremely disappointed in someone you trusted as a "God's person", just remember, is wasn't God who let you down and he can heal any damage caused by the situation. Jesus didn't blindly trust people and we shouldn't either. We are clearly told by reading in Matthew 7 what to look for in a leader. "Don't be impressed with charisma: look for character. Who preachers ARE, is the main thing, not what they say. A genuine leader will never exploit your emotions or your pocketbook."

Shortly after that, I got a job offer to move to Nashville. I had family there so it was a great opportunity. Life was good. I was pretty much over the whole church thing. Even though I was over the church thing God wasn't over me. His unseen and unacknowledged hand continued to protect me.

I connected with a guy from my past during visits back to my hometown. It was more of a long time high school crush than a healthy relationship. I was living with an attitude of doing whatever pleased me at the time. Doing it the *"right"* way sure hadn't worked. Letting a lack of good judgment get the best of me, I became pregnant.

Just before I was hit with that news, I had learned that Daddy was sick with emphysema. It was a big change for our family. Daddy had always been the provider and Mom was the homemaker. Now the tables had turned. Daddy was home on disability and Mom was looking to go to work to supplement finances. I had decided to move back to my hometown to do what I could to help through this transition. But I was pregnant! I went from having good intentions about moving home to being full of fear, shame, and embarrassment. The feelings of guilt and condemnation had already been securely planted in my life by the "God's person." I guess finally I had something I could rightly feel guilty and condemned about. How on earth could I bring a pregnancy home to my parents? They were going to be so disappointed in me. This was going to break their heart! I had already left my job to make the move. So not only was I between health insurance policies … but… I was pregnant!

The evening after I had taken the home pregnancy test I had gone out to eat with my parents. I remember it as clearly as if it were yesterday. We were standing in line at a fast food restaurant. I was wearing a red suit. It was probably a size five. The skirt was pencil straight while the top wrapped across my chest and was lined with a black border. I ran my hand across my tight flat stomach thinking this would be the smallest I'd probably see my core for a while. Fear was mounting inside with my news but a small light of hope flickered that the father of the baby would make things better or at least make the load lighter. After all, he certainly was no stranger.

The following day I shared the information with him. I am sure the shock and fear overtook him as well. His immediate answer was "I'm already a father (divorced), I don't want any more children and I don't want to get married. All I can offer is to pay for an abortion." Wow, that was a quick answer. That was the only participation he wanted or offered to have. I let fear paralyze me. I was afraid of the financial struggle, I was afraid of being alone, I was ashamed of myself, I knew people would talk about me but most importantly I didn't want to let my parents down and be a larger burden on them. The flicker of hope to face this situation had been abruptly doused with feelings of abandonment and hopelessness.

If I could have moved my mind away from the fear for just a moment, I would have known that the love in my family, my extended family, and my friends would have helped me to conquer anything. I certainly would have had support but I could not see that through the cloud of fear and feeling of abandonment. I'm sure that little life would have brought joy to us all. But no…I gave into the fear and made THE WORST decision of my life. I did not realize the HUGE effect this would have on my future. That decision would begin a downhill spiral that would continue for decades.

I vividly remember the trip to have the "procedure". It was entirely too easy. Looking back, I wish there had been some resistance somewhere along the way. I believe if there had been a couple of hurdles to jump I may have reconsidered that decision. Nevertheless, it all happened extremely fast.

Early the next morning I made a phone call to a clinic in Knoxville inquiring information. They were willing to 'see' me as soon as I could get there. I made a phone call to the father of the child hoping a night of thinking about the situation had brought a different answer. No change. He immediately rearranged his day and offered to drive and pay.

There wasn't a lot of conversation during the drive. Once we arrived, I was immediately taken from the waiting room down a long hallway then into a very drably painted room. It was cold and the atmosphere was dreadful yet everyone was very nice. It was so early in the pregnancy there wasn't even a heartbeat. The nurses did two blood tests to accurately determine that there was indeed HCG (human chorionic gonadotropin) present to verify the pregnancy. I was in there alone. The hopelessness I felt was darkness all around me and emptiness inside me. It was over as quickly as it began. My body reacted appropriately without any complications. Within thirty- six hours of a home pregnancy test, one phone call, and a couple hundred dollars, my life had changed forever.

After 'the procedure' we traveled back an old family farmhouse where the father was staying at the time. I remember being in a sleep that seemed I could not awaken from. It was mostly depression and not drugs that kept me down. Later that evening, I went home and began my life of living behind a mask. I may have had a couple more conversations with the father over the next few days. After that, it was about twelve years before we spoke again. We found ourselves at the same functions a couple of times during those years but purposely avoided each other.

It was a little secret I thought I could live with. Maybe it was a secret only two people knew about, but that little secret became something that constantly haunted me twenty- four hours a day. It seemed everywhere I went I was surrounded with newborns. In all honesty, it was probably no more than usual. I just noticed everything about each baby I saw. The cooing, the sweet little sounds, the smell of baby powder, the soft hair on their heads, the tiny little hands and feet, and the loving cuddles of mothers were all magnified.

I knew inside that I was the most horrible person on the earth. How could I have just had an abortion? That went against EVERYTHING I believed. Thank God, no one knew. Oh, but wait…God knows…of course, HE does. In my mind, I had just committed an unforgivable sin so my relationship with Him would be forever changed. I was already having feelings that He was against me but deep inside I had hoped I was wrong. I began living life as one person on the outside and another on the inside. My dark secret must remain hidden.

Trying to move forward, I named the baby. I read somewhere that was a step of healing for someone who had had an abortion or lost a baby. I felt like this baby was a boy so I picked the name Stefan Gabriel. Just in case I missed the gender, it could be Stephanie Gabriela. My baby had a name and my secret was safe.

I knew enough to know that my baby was in Heaven and in the arms of Jesus. I would try to focus on everything I had been taught in Sunday School about Heaven, eternity, and that glorious reunion one day. That truth was an anchor. Yet the storm of my guilt and condemnation was greater. Jesus may have my baby but I doubted I would ever make it there to hold him. Why is it we can so easily embrace condemnation, guilt, and shame yet struggle with forgiveness?

# 8

## MAYBE I NEEDED A CHILD— MAYBE HE NEEDED A MOM

Life in my hometown was not as easy to settle back into as I had hoped. Many of my friends were busy with their families and small children. Having grown up in church in this small town, not attending would draw attention and begin the questions. Why are you not going? What's wrong with you? I would have immediately been labeled a *backslider*. I knew the routines enough to cover my inner struggle in such a way that no one would know my hidden secret. I tried to go back to church one more time but the inner hypocrite ate at me each time I was there.

There were probably a couple of people I could have talked with about the worst decision of my life but I could not bring myself to do it. I kept up my outward façade. After all, I had just moved back from Nashville so I didn't have many friends in my hometown I was still tight with. It's easier to hide a secret when you are not close to anyone.

One girlfriend had been recently divorced. Her home was always graciously open to me and it became a regular hangout. Her daughter and son were between the ages of nine and twelve. Most every night became an opportunity to play games with the children. We loved board games and cards. I noticed that a child of one of her neighbors started hanging out with us regularly. This child, named Randall, was about ten years old. He was one of the most polite, respectful children I had ever encountered. After he went home one evening I learned that his mother was dying with cancer. His dad was spending so much time caring for his mom that my girlfriend had given them an open invitation for him to be at her house playing with her children. We included him in as many activities as we could like trips to Pigeon Forge to play mini golf or ride go carts. I became very attached to this little boy.

Within a few weeks, Randall's mother did pass. It was several weeks later before he returned to hang out with us. One evening his dad came to pick him up. Up until that time I had not met his dad because he had been busy caring for his wife. When this child introduced me to his father, he introduced me as *his girlfriend*. How precious was that????

His dad began hanging out with us too. It was early spring and we had a full season of warm weather to enjoy. To us, the winter months carried memories of the abortion and the death of a wife and mother. Budding trees, blooming flowers, days boating on the lake, and long hours of sunshine did not come quick enough. The dad had a certain fun competitive side to him. Heated competitions over a *Pente'* board became frequent events. The laughter we shared that summer was very therapeutic.

One evening we were going to meet at a local pizzeria for dinner. It ended up being just the three of us. We hit the weekly evening buffet with all the salad, pizza and spaghetti we could eat. I noticed that Randall was feeling a little down that night. He was very quiet and I could only imagine how this child must be missing his mom. Since laughter is the best medicine, it was time to have some fun.

I went to the bar and got two plates of spaghetti noodles and two straws. As I sat down I put a plate in front of me and a plate across the table in front of him. Randall wasn't really paying attention to what I was doing so I took the straw and sucked a noodle up in it. With all the air I had inside me, I blew that noodle across the table right into his face. His eyes doubled in size with surprise. He gave his dad a look as if to say, "Has this lady lost her mind?" I am not sure his dad had a clue what I was doing either so I blew another noodle even harder into this child's face. I gave him a look as if to say, "Are you going to take this?" and blew another noodle. He looked at his dad seeking permission to join in. Without missing a beat, I kept firing noodles. Finally, the fight was on. I had ignited the fire in that little boy and we began making the biggest mess I am sure that restaurant had ever seen. The other customers around us could not help but join in the laughter. Mission accomplished. He was having fun. Okay, it was at the restaurants expense but we made extra good with the bill and cleaned up the mess before we left.

Maybe these relationships were developing because three people were grieving in their own way. Maybe there was a void being filled between me and this little boy. Maybe I needed a child and maybe he needed a mom.

# 9

## PRAY FOR US— BROTHER DOPEY

At the same time, Daddy's health was slowly declining, but it wasn't life threatening. He had agreed to having an oxygen producing machine at home and taking portable tanks with him if he went out. He may have been losing some strength but his sense of humor was a strong as ever. We both were night owls and loved to sit up late watching TV and laughing. We could watch an episode of *Andy Griffith* that we had seen more than a dozen times, add our own sarcastic lines and laugh hysterically. Mom was adjusting to a career life she had never known. Plus, she always went to bed at a 'reasonable' hour. The bedrooms and living room were on the same floor in our small house. More nights than I care to remember, Daddy and I would get carried away laughing then suddenly hear a slamming door from down the hall. Oops!!! We would just look at each other knowing we had gone too far and gotten too loud.

Daddy had the nickname "Dopey" from the time he was a teenager. The stories I have heard is he got it when the movie *Snow White and the Seven Dwarfs* was released. Because of his sense of humor and silliness, "Dopey" stuck with him. Daddy was a straight A student and an All State football player. Several of the guys he played football with had stayed and made their lives in our hometown. It just so happened that most of them went to the same church and attended the same Sunday school class. Daddy had worked every Sunday for years but now that his Sundays were free they insisted he join them in that class.

I had the privilege of going with him one Sunday morning. His buddies had gone together and gotten him a large oxygen tank for the room so he would not have to bring his little portable ones. I didn't personally know many of his buddies even though I had gone to school with most of their children.

We sat reverently as the class opened. I had fully intended to be the quiet, supportive, respectful daughter and meet his friends. As the class began, one of his dearest buddies read the list of prayer requests. As he finished, he looked over at my Dad and said "Brother Dopey, would you lead us in prayer?" BROTHER DOPEY??? Are you kidding me? Well that was the first time I had heard that one. As Daddy started praying I started laughing. The more "Brother Dopey" prayed, the harder "Sister Debra" laughed. Have you ever been in that place where the most inappropriate thing to do was to laugh??? It only makes it worse. I was laughing so hard I was shaking my chair. Daddy just kept praying as if I wasn't sitting there beside him totally losing my composure. When he finished, I apologized to the class and told them I had never heard him referred to as ''Brother Dopey''. He was just Daddy to me. Everyone graciously laughed. I would sarcastically refer to him as "Brother Dopey" many times after that.

Even though my relationship with Daddy was one to be envied, it was not perfect. One of the barriers that was always between us was his chain smoking. It was rare that he was seen without an unfiltered cigarette in his hand. I hated the smell and I hated the sickness it eventually brought to his body.

Daddy was also a workaholic. He worked seven days a week at that little store. He would go in around 1-2pm every afternoon and work until 1-2am. Each morning when I left for school he was asleep and each afternoon when I returned he was at work. If I got to spend any time with him I had to work my way through customers, employees, and the business of the day. As I grew up, I spent more and more time there with him 'working'. I will forever be thankful for the work ethic and people skills he taught me. I have no doubt that part of the reason I was close to Eddie and Frank is because I shared Daddy with them.

The love between us was so much greater than these two flaws. Daddy always pulled himself away when I played basketball. I would look up from the court and see him standing there watching with his leg propped up and a cigarette in his hand. He rarely missed a game. He saw me cheer occasionally but wasn't nearly as committed to my cheerleading. However, regardless of the love we shared, in the home most of the time I had an absent father. I knew if I was doing anything from piano recitals, acting as the band drum major, playing basketball…etc. he would be there. I became very performance oriented. The more I performed, the more time I got with him.

If the only two things I can complain about are his smoking and working too much, I don't have a lot to complain about. I'm sure the 'absent' father contributed to my struggles in relationships with men. I knew I was loved and he was an excellent provider, but I did not grow up with a man in the house. He provided everything Mom and I needed and wanted, but she was left with the biggest part of the responsibility to raise me. She had her hands full because our personalities were completely different, but she sure stepped into the role she was handed.

# 10

## TWO WEEKS FROM BEING DIAGNOSED— I SAID GOODBYE

One afternoon, near the end of August 1991, Daddy got up from his chair with an unusually hard pain in his rib cage. I took him to Johnson City, TN to the VA hospital. We were told that he had cracked a rib, it would heal on its own, and we were sent home. On September 15th, 1991, he stood up again with the same pain on the other side. We assumed he had cracked another rib because he had been giving weight to that side to ease the pain of the first cracked rib. Back to the hospital we went. Mom was working. I called her and told her we were running up to the VA and would be back in time for dinner.

The broken rib was confirmed and they wanted to keep him for further tests. We spent the entire day going from one test to another. The VA was a teaching hospital so students and residents were in every area offering their help. We were told around 6pm that they wanted to admit him to continue tests the following day. As we were waiting for all that paperwork to happen, a student came in to look at Daddy's x-rays which were still hooked on the light box. He glanced at them for only a couple of minutes and looked at Daddy and said, "Mr. Hayes has your cancer spread?" CANCER??? SPREADING??? Heck, we were only dealing with a couple of broken ribs. What could he possibly be talking about? I immediately answered back and said, "Oh he doesn't have cancer, just a couple of broken ribs!" I wanted to finish by saying "You need to get back in class and learn to read x-rays before you verbally vomit!!!" Nevertheless, the C word was out and our mind had absorbed it. That was the quietest time I had ever spent with Daddy.

The student left and no one would answer any questions. All we were told was more test were lined up for the next day. I made the call to Mom to tell her they were keeping Daddy. We waited until she arrived before we told her about the student with the diarrhea of the mouth.

The next day the tests continued and continued AND continued. Daddy was his pleasant self with all the staff, being grateful for everything they did for him. Me, on the other hand, not so much. Someone had mentioned THAT word and no one would follow up with any explanations.

Finally, on Oct. 1 the doctors sat us down and gave us the results. Daddy not only had lung cancer but the cancer was also in his bones. Thus, the answer to the broken ribs. He was given one year to live. It was strongly suggested that he stay in the hospital for extended treatments. I believe he had a couple of rounds of radiation and the one year was quickly reduced to six months.

I was not leaving that hospital. Even though I made my living on commissions selling insurance, I was not going to let a dollar keep me from my Daddy. Life had drastically changed. I knew I was not the only person to hear this news and have their life changed forever by the C word. Now more than ever, I began thinking about Heaven.

I was processing the thoughts that I had a child in Heaven that Daddy didn't know about. What would he think of me once he met that child? Eternity just became real. During the following week, social workers tried to get me into their support groups. I had no interest but was finally dragged into one. I am not in any way bashing their intentions, but it did nothing for me at all. The questions I was dealing with in my mind could not be answered in a support group. It seemed to me that some of the people in that group had been long standing members still talking about their circumstances if they happened yesterday. I just kept thinking to myself, "I thought these groups were to help you move forward, not to continually rehash the same thoughts each session."

My Daddy was a strong Christian man by this time in his life. His approach to his death sentence offered strength not only to our family, but it was an inspiration to the staff as well. The cancer in his bones spread quickly. Within ten days his arm had broken. His answer to that was, "I am just falling apart." My fear was that his neck or back would break next.

One evening as I was sitting up with him he took my hand and said "Deb, God never promised us an easy flight, just a smooth landing." I don't know if those were his words or if he had heard them somewhere but they were forever written on my heart.

The *Atlanta Braves* were in the 1991 World Series. That was our team. We had made trips to Atlanta to see the *Braves* play. As we sat there watching the game, I knew in my heart it would be the last game we ever watched together. Daddy had fallen asleep but woke up to ask me for some ice and wanted to know how the *Braves* did. Those were the last words I would hear him say. I had spent the night in his room so Mom could get some sleep on a sofa in a waiting area. When the sun arose, we traded places so I could grab some sofa time. I went into the bathroom to change clothes and began to pray. (I was still relatively comfortable praying for other people just not so much for myself. I felt I had let God down in such a big way with the abortion that I didn't deserve to be asking for anything for me but I was confident asking for other people.) My prayer went something like this. "God, I don't want to live without my Daddy but it hurts too much to see him suffer. Please take him before his neck, back or other parts of his body break. I don't want to see him in all this pain. I know you have my baby and I know that Daddy will love him once he meets him." No sooner than I got those words out of my mouth Mom was knocking on the bathroom door. "Deb, I think he is gone, I think he is gone. Get out here". Sure enough, it appeared that Daddy was no longer breathing. We called the nurse, who in turn called a doctor to confirm that he had passed.

People I loved stood beside me, yet I felt more alone than I ever had in my life. I needed to take a walk by myself. I walked down the hall to the family area. As with most cancer units, there was a large room with many tables, puzzles, and plenty of things to occupy someone's time. The back side of the room was nothing but a wall of windows. I stood and stared out at the beautiful hillside of trees ablaze with the luminous colors of autumn. As I looked out that window something strange happened. I saw Daddy looking as young and healthy as I had ever seen him. He was holding the hand of a little boy that looked to be about six to seven years old. That little boy, my Stefan, had a full head of curly black hair. Both their faces were radiating with smiles. They looked at me then looked at each other and were gone. This all occurred within a matter of seconds. I'm not saying that I physically saw them but I will go to my grave believing that God let me see them in my spirit so I would know that they were together and all was okay. That was October 14, 1991. Two weeks from being diagnosed.... I said good bye.

# 11

## MY HEART MELTED—
## TO CALL HIM DADDY

The days following his death were busy and filled with an extreme outpouring of love and support. I knew Daddy had touched many lives in our hometown but I did not know to what extent. We had many people calling and coming by sharing stories. They told of how he had given them groceries when they were in need or bought something he had no need of from someone just to help them out of a tough spot. My heart melted to call him Daddy. To this day, I get inboxes on Facebook from people expressing how Daddy had touched their lives.

Our house was filled with a constant flow of family and friends. No sooner than we had gotten home from the hospital than two of my parents' closest friends, Buddy and Lou, were there with hugs, tears and food. Isn't it precious, how at a time like that, you seem to remember the first faces you see? Every gesture of love no matter how large or small during a time of loss is appreciated.

Daddy's funeral was as simple as the life he lived. The flow of friends and family at the funeral home lasted for hours. I was grateful for every face I saw and every hand I held. (Note to self: if you are ever in a receiving line wear comfortable shoes. Do not let the pain in your feet keep you from thanking someone for coming or hugging a neck. I was barefooted within thirty minutes). Most of the family was pleased and supportive of the choices we made for his funeral but let there be no doubt that when you break from traditions there will be some backlash.

The day we sat at the funeral home making his arrangements I began to reflect on other times I have been to viewings. I remember hearing people say things like" Don't they look good?" Or "They look so much younger." I know those remarks would be said with the sincerest intentions but I could only imagine that I would hear them for so long before I would come back with some sarcastic remark. I could already hear myself saying "No, he doesn't look good. How could my dead father in a casket be something that looks good to you?" Or "Seriously?? Don't you think if we all used a little embalming fluid our face would look much younger?" At that point, I decided to step outside of the box of tradition (for 1991) and ask Mom if we could have a closed casket. Being the sweet understanding soul that she is, after hearing my reasons she agreed. This did not sit so well with my grandmother who lived during the time that people sat up with dead people in their homes. I also got a lot of resistance from Daddy's brother. Nevertheless, I stood my ground and offered what I considered to be a good compromise. I would leave him open until the time for the visitation then have the funeral home attendants close him before I arrived. This would give anyone an opportunity to spend time there before he was closed and I would not have to see him nor hear those remarks all night.

I am only discussing these arrangements to remind people that the funeral and after death activities are ultimately for the ones left behind. Granted, it is a time to honor and celebrate the life of the one who has passed but it is done to bring closure for the ones still here. Do not be fearful to break from traditions to make this time more bearable or give honor to your loved ones in ways that have not been done before. It is nice to see that, from the time of Daddy's funeral to this publication, many traditional funerals have become customized celebrations of loved ones.

# 12

## BEETLEJUICE— CLIMBED ABOARD

Prior to the time of Daddy's diagnosed sickness and home going I had begun dating Randall's dad. We were becoming a little trio. Even though I was introduced as Randall's girlfriend, I eventually married his dad.

As a small boy, Randall loved history, the Civil War, and trains. A year before we were married we took him for a weekend in Chattanooga TN. He was so excited to go to the battlefields and explore the history related to that place. It was our first extended time together. At this point in his life, trains were the main attraction. Not just any trains, they had to be steam engines. And better yet, a Southern steam engine. While visiting the Tennessee Valley Railroad Museum we discovered there was a train excursion we could take passing through pre-Civil War Mission Ridge Tunnel which was completed in 1858. What an ecstatic little boy we had on our hands. When we got to the ticket counter we discovered that for a few dollars more we could buy a ticket to ride in the engine with the conductor. Well of course there was no question as to which ticket we were buying for Randall. He would be riding with the conductor. Tickets bought and we were headed for the train.

Seriously?? He had to be wearing long pants? It was summer, it was hot, we did not bring long pants for him and they were telling him he could not ride with the conductor. The look on the face of that child standing there in shorts broke my heart. He looked up at me with the most disappointed eyes I think I have ever seen. The practical side of me understood their policy because there were many opportunities for him to be burned in the engine. So, in his true Randall nature, even at that age, he was willing to quietly come back and take a seat with us in the passenger car. This temperament remained consistent throughout all the years I was with him. Ninety nine percent of the time he was willing to accept things not going his way without any fuss or complaining.

As we were turning away and moving toward the passenger car, I was digging deep inside my mind trying to find a solution that would put that child in the engine. I asked the attendant if it had to be blue jeans. He said no. I asked them how long we had until the train pulled out? With a few minutes to spare we headed to the parking lot. We dug through his luggage like a rat after cheese. Finally, found those *BeetleJuice* pajamas he loved. Right there in the parking lot…Off with the shorts and on with the pajama bottoms! I felt some satisfaction for succeeding at my first mommy test as we raced back to the train. *Beetlejuice* climbed aboard.

My relationships with that precious child and his dad were solid. I had encouraged his dad to follow his dreams and go to a school of higher education in another state. They both had moved a few months before Daddy was hospitalized. With Daddy gone, my life was empty and lonely. Even though, I had the urge to run, I held tight to the relationships with these two guys.

Granted, ideally, I would have fallen in love with the man first then added the child to the relationship, however, I had fallen in love with the child then the dad. I guess stranger things have happened to bring two people together. From the beginning of our dating relationship we shared lots of laughter and our friendship was strong. We stayed busy doing anything we could find to avoid sitting quietly with God and dealing with the pain we both carried inside. There was a definite void, but it seemed we could fill it with each other. One would think we were moving forward. What we had in common during the early days of our relationship was knowing how to escape and dodge the inner pain. Looking back, we both agreed we were happily numbing pain together.

It was so much easier to mask the pain inside than to deal with it. So, that is what we did. We just let the pain we had both recently experienced lay dormant. If we had taken the two years we knew each other prior to getting married and sought some practical healing, either our marriage would have made it through the future hurricane sized storms we faced or we would have realized our friendship was only to help each other through that rough season of life.

The rejection of Stefan's dad was still fresh and painful. Randall's father, wanted me. That was a twist. He knew about the abortion and still wanted me. He was different than anyone I had ever dated. I had always been with the athletic type. He was more into sci-fi than sports. The lake was our common ground instead of the tennis courts I had basically lived on for years.

I married Randall's father ten months after Daddy passed. It was working. I was a new wife, a new mother, living in a new place, starting a new job, and exploring new adventures. This marriage had a good beginning, but I have no problem saying if either of us would have had any clue of the storms we were going to weather we both would have immediately run the other way as fast we could.

I think that my tendency to run from a relationship had swung to the other side of the pendulum. I was now thinking that because of my relationship with this child I would make this work regardless of the cost.

# 13

## HURTING PEOPLE—
## HURT PEOPLE

All relationships have struggles, disagreements, and challenges. We were no exception. Amidst the laughter, we had big fights. There were three huge ones that left holes in my heart. The first was while we were dating, the second was the night before the wedding and the third was about a year and a half into the marriage. I am not including these in any way to toss blame but only to show how the unresolved pain reared its ugly head. It triggered our insecurities, stubbornness, selfishness, and fear of the uncertainty of the future.

Both the guys had moved to Ohio before Daddy passed. Randall's dad had enrolled in school to fulfill his lifelong dream of becoming a photographer. Little One was settling into elementary school. My mind had been in a fog with Daddy. The suddenness of his diagnosis and passing carried with it what was becoming a familiar measure of shock. I was busy with Daddy's arrangements and spending time with several out of town family members. Due to school schedules, the guys were not going to be able to make it back to town for Daddy's viewing.

I am not even sure what started the fight but did we ever have one big one the night before Daddy's visitation. The conversation revolved around who I expected to see at the funeral home, referring to my old flames. Words exploded. I am not sure where these insecurities were coming from. Knowing my history of running, his question I guess could have been a reasonable one. What I would do in my vulnerable state of mind if old flames showed up? And that was a very real possibility in such a small town. Then again, the concerns about old beaus and the fear of losing me were most likely symptoms resurfacing from the unresolved pain of recently losing his wife. None the less, after being pressed on the issue for a lengthy time, that bird wasn't flying with me.

I was living through the most dreaded time of my life. I was on edge and I tend to become sarcastic when I am fearful or stressing. I was going to be saying goodbye to my Daddy and trying to be hospitable to hundreds of people in the process. If he really kept crossing that line with old flames I was ready to say goodbye to him too. I am sure I didn't hold back my smart mouth letting him know just how I felt. "Just stay in Ohio and don't even bother coming down for the funeral if you need to critique the crowd and my reaction to it."

That was a perfect example of hurting people hurting people. In his efforts to be protective of me, the insecurities of losing me took top billing. I could only see a man trying to control me. I had just lost the only man that I fully trusted and here was another one in the middle of my personal space trying to tell me how to handle it.

That fight was the largest of several we had between the time Daddy passed in October and becoming engaged in December. Both he and I have recently admitted the fights exposed underlying pain that we should have paid attention to. The problems were inside ourselves not with each other. Yet, we planned to marry and make my move to Ohio in July. Again, maybe I was numbing more pain by planning a wedding as therapy.

# 14

## DO I CHOOSE MY FIANCE'— OR CLEAN HAIR?

Another large fight occurred the night before we were married. As with most weddings as the day drew nearer the stress thickened. Flowers, food, music, attendants, dresses, tuxes…etc. At least I didn't have to concern myself with the photography. The groom was going to be the photographer! What?? Are you kidding me?? I wasn't exactly sure what that looked like but I was somewhat relieved when he admitted he was bringing an assistant. The wedding became more of a production than an intimate time of passionate pledges and vows. Long distance planning was hard enough but add to it Mom's disappointment with me moving out of town again.

She would be completely by herself for the first time ever. She was going through all the motions of participating in showers and parties and doing all the right things. However, she had boldly declared she would not be attending the wedding. Her only child was moving three hundred miles away only ten months after her husband had passed. Sometimes there just seems to be no right answers that please everyone. I wish I hadn't been an only child but I was. I wish the direction of my life was to stay in our hometown but it wasn't. Fortunately, at that time, she had several siblings living and I knew she would not be alone. They would be there and take care of her. Her oldest sister did intervene for me and informed her that she WOULD be attending my wedding. (She did. In fact, she walked me down the aisle.)

All the parties were behind me. Mom was on board. Friends and family were coming in from out of town. All my ducks were in a row. Well, not exactly! The dresses had become a living nightmare. The seamstress had taken so many shortcuts and procrastinated to the last minute. My dress was beyond altering. I had taken her a picture of a dress with a beautiful sheer turtle neck. It was bordered with beads and pearls. What I got was a high scoop with lace. I looked like my head was popping out of the middle of a daisy.

We exhausted all resources and found other seamstresses to finish the bridesmaids' dresses the night before the wedding. We were frantically collecting and refitting dresses following the rehearsal dinner.

Earlier that day the seamstress had held the bridesmaid's dresses hostage and would not release them to be remade. Yet the workmanship was so poor they were unsuitable to be worn. In her haste, she had put emerald green zippers into deep teal dresses as well as left strings hanging from top to bottom. I wrote her a check to claim the dresses and redistribute them for proper alterations. From there I made a beeline to the bank to put a stop payment on the check. That crap hit the fan and we ended up in court a few weeks later, which I won with little effort.

For a lady who was not going to the wedding Mom sure stepped inside this mess and got it resolved at the very last minute. What a fiasco!! (Note to self and anyone else remotely interested in planning a wedding…BUY THE DRESSES… do not try to save money having them made regardless of references.)

The photographer/groom was also stressing. To get the pictures he wanted, I had agreed to shoot all the formals before the wedding. At that point, who cared about the tradition of not seeing each other on the wedding day?

The stress escalated and so did the words between us. While I was running the race of finishing bridesmaid's dresses, I received an annoying phone call. He was upset that I didn't make time to be alone with him. That would have probably been the proper thing to do but this wedding had become a production and the dress disaster had taken all my time and attention. I was thinking that we had the rest of our lives together and that my priority was to make sure the details of the wedding came together.

We had another HUGE BLOWOUT of words. Quite honestly, I wasn't even sure he was going to show up at the wedding. When we hung up the phone I had no assurance that we were getting married the next day. I was given a demanding ultimatum to give him one hour of private time the next morning or it was off.

The wedding day came. I debated whether to meet him and go forward or completely be a NO SHOW for the entire day. I didn't have an appointment to get my hair done. I liked doing it myself. The uncertainty of the day overtook me as I looked in the mirror on the morning of what should have been one of the happiest days of my life. Within the time frame I was working under, I could either meet the requirement of the Groom or take the time I needed to do my hair. I could not do both. Quite frankly, I was too tired to care what my hair may or may not look like for a day that may or may not happen. So, I thought again of Randall and opted not to wash my hair and meet the Groom.

We had taken formal bridal pictures weeks before the wedding. He shot them in a lovely setting with a stained-glass backdrop at the Dayton Art Institute. The surroundings were so beautiful no one would notice the lack of beadwork on the back of the dress. (Plus, my hair was perfect that day.) Knowing we already had those pictures was a contributing factor in the decision to have breakfast with the groom on the day we were to be wed.

The photos with the bridal party were to begin at 1:00 pm that afternoon. The ceremony wasn't until 6:30 pm that evening. He had scheduled each group a time slot for pictures. The pictures began with the bride and groom together then added the other attendants throughout the afternoon. Their patience was to be admired! We did provide snacks but admittedly it was a long afternoon for all. All the pictures were completed before the wedding began except for the grandmothers. Quickly after the ceremony we grabbed a couple of pictures with them. Mission accomplished!! Pictures complete!! Yes....in every picture my bangs were separated where my dirty hair had parted.

We ventured to a quaint little neighboring town to begin the honeymoon at an old historic Inn. However, the old historic air conditioner had quit working so we enjoyed our wedding night in approximately 110 degrees. We attempted to continue the honeymoon in Gatlinburg. While sitting by one of the mountain streams in Cades Cove, we talked about how familiar it all was and that it just didn't seem special. The mountains were indeed romantic unless you had grown up there. The familiarity had become routine. I looked at the husband and said, "I'm ready to go home." Being relieved that I meant Ohio, he packed us up and we continued the honeymoon at Kings Island! Let life in Ohio begin!

# 15

## IT HAPPENED ONE TIME—
## SHOCKED AND SCARED

I was a new wife, a new mom, living in a new city, starting a new job and making new friends. Life was fresh. I worked full time while the husband had a small part time job cleaning the church twice a week between his school classes. Money was tight but we were hopeful. There were lots of festivals and activities going on so we attended as many as possible.

Oh, and of course now we had time to view the lovely wedding pictures. They were indeed good of everyone one who had taken the time to wash their hair that day. Being married to a photographer was like being married to a plumber and always having a leaky faucet in the house. Most brides got a book of proofs. (That was before digital photography.) It made no sense to the photographer to spend money making a proof book when I had contact sheets and loops. Right? For those of you who have no idea what that is, it is when all negatives are developed onto a sheet of paper as strips of film. You would have two or three strips of pictures on an 8 x10 sheet. Each picture was barely one inch by one inch. You would then take a 10X magnifying loop that is about the size of your eye to look at each picture closely to determine the ones to be printed. Granted, my dirty hair looked much nicer in the smaller pictures.

Randall was growing up fast and attending middle school. Our relationship was deepening and I was embracing being the mother of a pre-teen. Trains were still his top interest. Our apartment didn't offer a good place to set up his train track and all the village pieces that went with it. Instead, we made a track near the ceiling in his bedroom. He could lay in his bed and watch the train continuously loop around the top of his room.

One evening the dad and I had a dispute over what was a significant amount of money at the time. It had been spent without discussion. I thought we were saving for a couple of pieces of furniture because we were currently using those old three- foot high stereo speakers for end tables. But, he had *invested* in an authentic first generation autographed *Star Trek* plaque that should be worth a lot of money one day. We could not have been in more different corners concerning this purchase. Neither of us were giving in. Tempers and voices were escalating. We were upstairs in the bedroom and before I knew it he had pushed me on the bed. He was bent over me with his hands clinched tightly around my throat. I must have been able to let out a loud scream as it happened because immediately Randall ran into the room. I was terrified! I couldn't breathe! I don't know where this child got his strength. Maybe it was adrenaline. He pulled his dad off me and threw him towards the floor and told me to run. I pulled myself up, ran out of the room and quickly down the stairs.

I can honestly say I was traumatized. I had never heard my parents argue, much less have any physical contact. I was so scared I wanted to go straight back home to Tennessee that night. I knew with one phone call I could have family members making a trip to Ohio to "rescue" me. But I could not leave Randall. He had already lost one mother. I was not going to walk out on him.

It was a seemingly small issue that triggered a huge release of dammed up emotions. Years later when we looked back on that day and calmly discussed it, we discovered the underlying issues and thoughts that triggered it. We were both like ice bergs. The unresolved pain we brought into the marriage had received additional layers of unspoken issues. What was under the surface was growing inside us. That ignored pain was greater than the circumstances. We could have successfully resolved the issue of an undiscussed purchase. However, our layers of agony were screaming louder than reason.

The husband was still in school and I was carrying the burden of the finances. My job was located forty- five minutes south of our previous home. I worked until at least 10pm. One evening I was stuck in traffic with minor car trouble about 11pm. No car trouble is ever pleasant but being alone in a large unfamiliar city was very unnerving. The following day at work the conversation came up about moving closer. It made perfect sense to me. My late-night drives would be less time, it would be closer to the husband's school, and Randall would be changing schools the next school year anyway. I found a nice townhouse and talked to the husband about moving. Even though he agreed, he never expressed that he resented that I had taken the initiative with a co-worker to find an apartment.

That layer of resentment, atop the pain brought into the marriage, was his breaking point. When I confronted him about the *Star Trek* plaque he snapped. He has since said that it felt like an out of body experience for him. He knew he lost control and I was the object of his violent release.

Years later we verbally worked through that explosion. But at the time, it was not discussed at all. I believe the entire scene shocked and frightened us both. It honestly never happened again but for me it forever changed intimacy with him.

That wall around my heart went right back up. I began sleeping on the couch every night. I couldn't get to sleep in the same bed after that incident happened. If anyone asked why I slept on the couch, I would always say it was because of his snoring. Not only did that choking scene change intimacy, it affected communication throughout the rest of our marriage. I always felt I had to be aware of where the line of anger was that I could not cross when discussing issues. If there was ever a next time, Randall may not be around to intervene.

One of the sweetest cards I received from Randall was shortly after this incident. Reward cards were new to the scene. Such as, buy ten ice cream cones and get the next one free. Randall was an excellent artist. He enjoyed drawing or painting the cards he gave me. This one melted and broke my heart on so many levels. He used water colors on this card and stapled a rewards card he made inside it. The rewards were for seven exchanges of nights on the couch. Any night I wanted, I could give him the card and he would sleep on the couch while I slept in his bed. WOW!! What a precious child! What child should ever be put in that position?

That card holds significance on many levels. First, Randall drew it. Secondly, the mountains represent the place of my birth and the place I go to find peace when life gets rough. Thirdly, it reminds me of the love of a child when my trust in someone was betrayed. I relate that to the love of Jesus. He came to us as a child and reaches out to us in our darkest days. He not only comes with the words "I Love You", he wants to get involved in our most basic and practical needs.

I still carried the guilt from the abortion so in my mind I was beginning to believe that I deserved anything that went wrong in my life. I believed if I was mistreated in any way it was only a small taste of what I really deserved. Once this line of thinking embeds itself in your brain, it becomes more difficult to stand up for yourself.

# RISE

Happy
Birthday!

OFFICAL
couch
credit
card

Deb thank you for
all of your support as a mother
and a friend, I know that
I haven't always been the
best son but I have
always loved you.

your son
Randall

P.S. This card is good for
7 nights off swapping out for the couch!

# 16

## EPHRAIM IS ON THE WAY— APRIL 28, NOT A GOOD DAY

Almost three years after we were married I was pregnant with another little boy. Our marriage had become routine but we were moving forward. I had settled into being the mom of a young teenager and now the dream of having an infant in the family was coming true. We had chosen the name Ephraim, not only because it was a cool name, but it had reference to a second son. I loved every time I threw up. I loved every inch that my clothes became too tight. I loved each day I felt sluggish. I loved feeling that little guy move inside me. I loved knowing our family was growing.

Although thoughts of Stefan never left my mind I was beginning to feel more complete. Life was moving forward. The regrets were still strong but I was beginning to let forgiveness creep into my spirit.

April 28 1995....Not a good day!! I began having some cramps in my stomach. They weren't extreme but as any pregnant woman would, I had the husband take me to the doctor to be examined. The doctor checked the baby's heartbeat. It was strong. She checked my cervix and it was tightly closed. No worries. It was most likely something I ate. We left feeling relieved.

We were half way between the doctors' office and our home and the cramps began again. This time they were so intense I was doubled over in the car seat. Their timing was very consistent. I knew that we were in trouble. The husband made a u turn and headed immediately for the ER. In less than one hour from the time we left the doctor's office I was holding my lifeless little Ephraim in my arms. The shock I had become all too familiar with had rested on me again. I looked at this tiny stillborn baby, tears running down my face and my first thought was this was yet another payback for my mistake with Stefan.

The doctor had been paged for the emergency. She came running in the door screaming "I can't believe this I JUST examined her". The nurse took the baby to clean him. Upon examination of his little body, it was discovered that we had experienced something called Valamentous Cord Insertion. That was a situation where the umbilical cord inserts into the fetal membranes rather than the body of the placenta. This occurs in about one percent of single pregnancies and about eight to nine percent of twin pregnancies. ONE PERCENT OF SINGLE PREGNANCIES!!!!!! Think about those numbers. REALLY???? ONE percent. Of course, we were reassured that because it was such a rare occurrence we would have no problem conceiving another healthy child. That was a comforting thought, but at the time it meant very little when all hopes and dreams were lost for my son I had just delivered.

Ephraim was brought to me in his little blanket and cap. As the female doctor stood beside my bed, the M.D. kicked out and the mother kicked in. She and I made pictures and examined his little body. This baby had long legs and long fingers. Yes, he would have been a tall guy. I knew I was holding either a keyboard or basketball player. I will never have the answer to that question while here on this earth.

It is amazing sometimes the details you remember. This female doctor was covering for my regular doctor when Ephraim was born. She could have been the twin of a good friend of mine whom I had lived with for a while. She didn't just look like her, they had the same mannerisms. She had dark hair and wore it clipped back the exact same way. Even though I was living through a nightmare, the familiarity I felt with this doctor was bringing a soothing comfort. I wasn't entirely angry with God, but I sure was doubting him. Those doubts kept me from seeing it, but it was no coincidence that the

Dr. who looked exactly like one of my most comforting friends was filling in at the exact time I had to say good-bye to my Ephraim. I believe now that God loves us so much he does little things like that to console us. Oftentimes, however, they go unnoticed.

Later that evening we began making those dreadful phone calls to relatives and friends telling them the disappointing news. Giving the details over and over was not the way I wanted to end that day. The husband had gone to get Randall. Our friends had begun to show up at the hospital. When would this nightmare end?

If he had been born two weeks later, we would have received a death certificate instead of a miscarriage certificate. I realize the hospital has regulations but I was insulted that I got a miscarriage certificate when I clearly was holding my son in my arms and taking pictures with him. We were not offered the opportunity to have a funeral for him because it was a "miscarriage".

I was released the following day. The longest drive we ever made was pulling out of the parking lot and turning down the street toward home. The hospital is an attractive building that looks somewhat like a very nice hotel at the entrance. The street was lined with beautiful budding trees. As we drove down the street I felt like I was inside a dark room looking out a window into a world I could not touch. Much like the mole at the beginning of this book. I had ridden up the lane the day before with little Ephraim inside me but now I was riding down the same lane physically and emotionally empty.

Fortunately, the furniture for the nursery had not arrived, so upon returning home all I had to do was put baby clothes in a box for safe keeping. I found some peace in the rarity of the occurrence. After all, I was not the only person who had lost a baby. Now I had two little boys in Heaven with Daddy. Eternity was growing larger in my heart with each deposit made into Heaven. There is truth to the scripture that says Where your treasure is there your heart will be also. Ironically, I remember saying when I got married that one of my biggest regrets was that Daddy would not know my children nor would they know him. Little did I know, he would get know them long before I would.

# 17

## TIME TO LAUGH—
## HERE COMES ISAAC

Life was good again!! We had allowed ourselves to move forward. I had focused my thoughts on being thankful that my life had been blessed with Randall. I felt privileged being his mom. We were surrounded by a wonderful group of people at our church and work who encouraged us and kept us focused on the future. A few months had past and I was pregnant again without any problems.

Yes, it was time to laugh and start enjoying this life. It was fitting that our little "Isaac" was growing inside me. Hope had overcome fear and disappointment.

Randall was sixteen. He continued to be extremely supportive. I don't believe his enthusiasm was as high for being a big brother as it was for his truck and driving freedoms. He was involved with a civil war reenactment group. One of our dear friends was in the group so we knew he was safe and well taken care of when he would venture away with them. I was learning to let go with Randall and at the same time looking forward to cradling a new infant.

Our condo was filled with congratulatory cards and flowers to celebrate this happy season. One of my favorite things was to take Randall's hand and place it on my belly to let him feel Isaac move. His response would be to smile and give me a look that implied, "Don't you dare do this with or in front of my friends."

One quiet afternoon I was enjoying my time alone at home with a carefree mind and peaceful spirit. I noticed I had some spotting when I went to the bathroom. Although I didn't panic, I knew I was not going to take any chances. I tried to find the husband. This was before cell phones were the primary means of communication. I could not locate him and I didn't want to make Randall uncomfortable with the issue. I called a close co-worker that had become like family. Immediately Brenda and her step-daughter Lisa were there to take me to the ER. Driving up the lane to the hospital brought back the memories of Ephraim. This was May 1996. The landscape was just as lively with fresh spring blooms as it was the year before. I knew this was going to be fine. After all Ephraim was a one percenter. I would get checked out, maybe put on a little bed rest, go back home and be back in a few weeks to deliver Isaac and take him home.

As I lay in that same emergency room, the doctor looked at me during the examination and said, "Sweetheart, your cervix is opening and the sac of water is beginning to protrude. You are not allowed on our feet until this baby is born." We needed to keep the little fellow inside the womb for at least three more weeks before he could be admitted to a NICU. I was immediately transported to the maternity ward and hooked up to numerous monitoring devices for both myself and Isaac. Within a few hours, the cervix had opened a little more. I was told that my water would break soon and I would deliver him that night.

This CANNOT be happening AGAIN!!!! Sure enough, my water broke but no contractions began. I kept laying on my back staring at the ceiling. Isaac was moving, his heart rate was fine. Twenty-four hours later, I am still laying there with a baby moving inside me. The doctors have turned their complete death sentence into hope that if things remained the same a few more weeks, he could be born. They were telling me that water was beginning to accumulate again.

I memorized every single tile on the ceiling to occupy my thoughts while holding that little one inside. There were pleasant interruptions of my tile counting when one of my dearest friends,

Cindy, would stop by. She always had a way of getting me to laugh even during the most dreadful of times.

Day after day went by. Two weeks later we were almost in the safe zone. I began feeling feverish. Keep in mind that I had to be totally on my back the entire time which meant I had to have assistance using bed pans. I was laying with a partially open womb and my fever had begun to climb. It became apparent that I had an infection. Soon afterwards Isaac's heart rate began to decrease. He was also getting the infection. If he had been born at that time, there would be no chance of survival and would not even be taken to the NICU. My body was getting weaker by the hour. The doctors were talking to me about inducing labor and beginning medications. Hemoglobin count was climbing to seventeen. It had been staying in a normal range of around twelve to fifteen. The doctors were telling me that I was beginning to endanger myself by not inducing labor.

There was no way I was giving them permission to induce labor knowing that my little Isaac was not going to survive. The all too familiar shock was back again. The only thing going through my mind was my baby was dying. I had no thoughts for myself, the husband or Randall.

Hemoglobin was now twenty- one. The doctors had brought the husband into the mix telling him that he would lose a wife and a son if he did not convince me to induce. He needed to do something quick!! He told them I was the priority, but I was not listening to him either. All I could think of was Daddy in Heaven with Stefan, Ephraim and soon he would have Isaac too. Why would I not want to join them? I was so beaten down I didn't care if I lived out any more time on this earth or not. NO!! I was not going to induce labor!

About the time I had made that loud proclamation, the contractions began. My weak body went into natural labor. The labor didn't last long but was very intense. Soon I had Isaac in my arms. He was a very sick little boy all cradled in his blanket and little cap, but he was alive.

Here came the meds. I didn't get to keep Isaac in my arms any length of time before the staff began pumping medication to fight my infection. I was too weak to hold him so the husband held him by my side so I could see him. I realize that the medical staff did the correct thing by beginning to fight for my life, but I had a dying child within eyesight. They gave me medication to make me sleep. That was NOT the time to sleep.

Isaac didn't have the long legs and fingers that Ephraim had. He probably would not have been as tall as his brother. His little (big) nose was just like mine and Daddy's. I was awake long enough to remember seeing his little heart beating through his thin skin. It was obvious that it was getting slower and slower. The husband sat beside me and held our son for an hour before he joined his brothers.

# 18

## HE PLANTED ETERNITY IN
## THE HUMAN HEART—
## I GET IT

I was fighting for my life. The antibiotics, pain medicine and whatever else they were pumping into me kept me in a daze. I was admitted to another room that was not on the maternity ward for recovery. Just about the time I felt my head had begun to clear, some people came in with information about a burial for Isaac. I had been able to hold his little body again and had already said my final goodbye. Who were these people wanting to talk to me about his burial? Now the confusion was climbing.

With Ephraim, I had thought the appropriate thing to do was to give him a funeral, but was never given that option. I had just assumed Isaac would be handled the same way since it was the same hospital. No, not this time! I had a certificate of death not miscarriage. (In spite, of the fact, that I held both boys and have pictures with each of them).

It didn't take long to see dollar signs add up as I looked through the paper work I was given. There obviously was no insurance on the baby. The cost quoted for the funeral was astronomical in addition to the cost of getting his little body back to Tennessee for his final resting place. It became over whelming fast.

However, the predominate factor in the thought process was that I was too sick to make the trip to a local funeral home, much less, a six- hour drive to Tennessee. I was drowning in confusion.

Would it be disrespectful not to have a funeral? How could I have a resting place for Isaac when I didn't have one for Ephraim? I didn't want people who didn't know my son to bury him when I was the one who carried him. Neither my body nor emotions were in any position to be making those decisions.

That was Memorial Day weekend. The husband's brother and his wife had made plans to spend that weekend with us. They continued with their plans. This pulled my husband away from the hospital and back to the house to entertain them. The thoughts and decisions I was trying to process alone became more than I could deal with. I asked the nurses to post a "no visitors" sign until I could talk to our pastor. He had proven to be a sincere "God's person" in my life and I needed him to sort through the tornado of thoughts twisting through my head.

He once again came through with wisdom and seeds of eternity. He explained the truth that the babies were already in the arms of Jesus. All three of my boys were probably playing together as we sat crying in the hospital room. They were happy and no doubt looking forward to the day Mommy would join them forever. All I had here on earth was the shell of Isaac's body. The decision I made at that point needed to be what was best for me. The husband had already told me that he would support whatever I wanted to do.

I couldn't do for one baby what I had not done for the other. I couldn't let family members bury my child when I couldn't be there. Tearfully, I asked the hospital to do with Isaac's body what they had done with Ephraim. There was just no right decision.

For many years, I doubted that decision when I would see others go to the graves of their babies. In the end, I did what was best at that time. Maybe I don't have markers here on this earth, but I have a movie of eternity playing daily in my mind. My babies are alive and in Heaven. This book will be my memorial of all my children who live and wait for me there.

Ecclesiastes has always been one of my favorite books in the Bible. But when I read in Chapter 3 verse 11 TLB "He has planted Eternity in the human heart", I had a deeper meaning of exactly what that meant.

# 19

## I JUST DID THAT?— I CUSSED OUT THE PASTOR?

The days of recovery were long and hard after Isaac was born. Both my body and emotions were fighting against me. The infection had left me struggling to walk. Once I got home from the hospital and made the trip up the stairs, I was there for weeks. My Mom and sister in law came to Ohio to care for us. Depression had set in. I had gone from the heights and anticipation of a newborn in our family to holding a lifeless baby in my arms AGAIN. I couldn't care less if I recovered or not. My thoughts had turned against God. I was totally convinced that he was a thief and had taken my babies. I would be forever living in the shadow of that abortion. Don't tell me God forgives and forgets. Obviously, he hadn't forgotten about Stefan or he would have let me keep at least one of my babies. I was beyond anger.

How could the loss of two infants thirteen months apart be so different? With Ephraim, it was primarily disappointment, but hope remained. Isaac felt like a slap in the face from God. He must have been out to humiliate me. The primary emotion I felt as I spoke to people about Isaac was embarrassment. Only a few months had passed since I was having these same conversations about not bringing Ephraim home from the hospital. Once wasn't enough. I didn't get knocked down far enough with Ephraim? I felt as if God was saying, "No, let's take Isaac too then she is sure to feel the pain." That may sound rough and raw but that is exactly where my thoughts were. I later learned I was in good company with thoughts like this. In Psalms 69 David is talking to God and saying, "Because of you I look like an idiot, I walk around ashamed to show my face". Granted, David was not talking about the death of a baby. The point is, he was not afraid to express his emotions to God. My paradigm was that God had taken the babies. I blamed Him for the embarrassment I was feeling. I later learned that was not the case but I developed a great appreciation for David's bold conversations with God in the Psalms. He wasn't afraid to be transparent and open with his thoughts. We will dig deeper into this in Part Four.

After a while my Mom and sister in law went home. I slowly got up and down the stairs, but all I wanted to do was lay on the couch. Both the husband and Randall were very helpful and supportive. Randall had his truck and was enjoying driving around with his friends. We were close enough that he continued to make time to hang out with me. One of our favorite shows to watch together was *Teletubbies*. (Save the judgement here. I know it was a little strange that a teenage son and his mom watched *Teletubbies*, but we did. And we enjoyed it.) My favorite was *La-La*. She was the yellow one. Randall called me *La-La* quite often before Isaac was born. *La-La* lived in her own happy little world and lollygagged around singing LA LA LA LA LA LA…. During one of my full- blown depression days on the couch, Randall came in with a stuffed yellow *La-La*. You could squeeze her tummy and she would repeat all her favorite sayings. I guess it was his way of trying to get me back to the *La-La* he once lived with instead of the Debbie Downer he currently lived with.

I loved him with all my heart but I was having anger issues with God as to why He wanted me to raise someone else's son but would not let me have one of my own. I didn't regret one minute of my time with Randall, but I was dealing with a hidden resentment that I couldn't raise my own sons also.

It wasn't Randall's fault that we couldn't keep his little brothers. It wasn't his fault he was now living with a depressed mother. Where did those thoughts come from? It seemed I could not stop the thoughts, yet I hated myself for even having them. I was caught in the gulf between having a teenager that was beginning

72

to experience independence and the Empty Arms Syndrome of two infants I could not hold. My thoughts and emotions were running wild. I purposely tried not to let him see any of the struggle inside me. I loved that boy with all my heart.

Randall was involved with the youth group at our church. The youth pastor had been there for less than a year and was such a sincere gentleman. He was great with the kids and Randall thought the world of him. One afternoon I was home alone partaking in a pity party where I remained the star. The youth pastor called to ask how I was doing. He did not deserve what he got on the other side of the phone.

"Are you kidding me? Just how do you think I am doing? Let's just not kid each other about that crazy God we say we serve. And the last thing I want you to do is try to quote me some scripture especially Romans 8:28. Don't even bring that one up. And no, I'd rather you not pray for me, thank you. Let me ask you, if God makes himself out to be such a healer then tell me why he couldn't heal at least one of two innocent babies." I added a few other choice words. He kindly tried to reassure me and hung up. I wonder if they taught him how to deal with hurting cussing church members in Bible School? Regardless, he handled it with caring professionalism.

Within minutes, I got a phone call from the Senior Pastor. Oops, was I in trouble? I didn't really care. No, he didn't call to correct me for cussing at the youth pastor. He said he was going to be in the area and asked if it would be okay to stop by. About an hour later he arrived at the condo. The first thing out of his mouth was "Don't worry. I left my Bible in the car. We aren't going to talk Scripture and I am not going to pray with you. I have already prayed for you." I was cool with that. He encouraged me to get all my anger out. If I wanted to cuss that was okay (for the moment) to get it out. God knew what was in my heart anyway. We talked a little chit chat then began to focus once again on the fact that God Is Good. Did I still believe that God was good? Well, NO I didn't. How could I believe that about the one who took my two babies?

He tried to tell me that God wasn't the one who took them. God was good. Unfortunately, while we live on this cursed ball of dirt called Earth, bad- things will to happen. Bad- things happen to good people very day. Life happens to us all. He encouraged me to try to begin focusing my thoughts once again on the fact that God was good. Try to at least look at the good things that are in my life instead of the losses I had just experienced. Well, God might be good but this sure didn't feel good.

We are back to the verse in John 10:10 that says "A thief is only there to steal and kill and destroy. I came so they can have real and eternal life, more and better life than they ever dreamed of." At first I interpreted this to mean that the thief was the one who took my babies. After much thought, I realized that was giving too much credit to our enemy. Life simply happens to everyone. I have no answers to why certain things happen to certain people or why unpleasant events seem to keep happening to the same people. What I do know is that where the enemy begins to steal, kill and destroy is with our thoughts. If he can distort our view of God, we can take care of destroying the abundant life God intended us to have all on our own. This realization came over years. At the point when Isaac went to Heaven I was still thoroughly convinced that God had taken them from me because of my mistake with Stefan.

Before the Pastor left he said something that really inspired me. It was like a lightbulb beginning to glow in a dark room. He said in passing, "Why don't you find something you have never done and learn to do it? That will challenge your mind to move forward instead of staying stuck in the current pain."

By then, my body had begun to recover and I had been working again but only part time. I would still get weak after being on my feet for any length of time but I was getting stronger. I laid on the couch that night and went to sleep pondering what Pastor had said about finding something new to learn. About 4AM I went upstairs and woke the husband up. "I've got it. I want to buy a motorcycle". Maybe Pastor was thinking more like arts and crafts, but I had just had a spring of excitement well up inside me. I needed to learn to ride a motorcycle. Yes, I needed a motorcycle to pull me from the pit and put me on the road to living again.

# PART TWO
## CRAWLING

*"I know I so often doubt you,*
*but you don't turn away when I'm about to"*

Collin Raye, "Undefeated'

# 20

## FOCUS YOUR SIGHT—
## GET SOME TRACTION

C rawling is an interesting thing. It means to move or progress slowly and laboriously, to move in a prone position as a worm or caterpillar. Before babies begin to crawl, they are usually lying on their backs much like a turtle turned upside down on its shell. They are going nowhere. It isn't until they are turned in a position where they can focus their sight toward something and begin to get some traction with their limbs that they can progress toward movement. As small children begin to crawl it is not uncommon for them to wobble and fall. They bring themselves to balance before they begin to move. Often, we see them land on their little bellies as they move forward. They lay there kicking their legs and feet as if they were waiting on encouragement to begin again. Other steps in the progression of movement are *sitting* then beginning to *rise*. I have never seen a child try to stand or begin to walk without hitting the ground a few times. Sometimes it is a simple bump and other times it is a hard thump that leaves them wounded or crying. It takes determination and encouragement to complete the task from *crawling* to *rising*.

Our healing is the exact same way. We begin in a position that feels like we are on our back and completely helpless. The circumstances that have knocked us down seem to be a weight holding us there. Even after we turn ourselves over and begin to focus on what may be in front of us, life can be wobbly. There are often things as simple as a thought, a song, or a special memory that triggers the emotions of the pain. We then relive it one more time. If life would just stop until we got it back together, it would make the process much easier.

I have seen music videos where the singer is moving through a crowd of people that are frozen in time. What a perfect scenario! But unfortunately, life keeps coming at us. We usually must function back into our careers. Oftentimes, we have other children that deserve our one hundred percent. Our crawling experience toward healing becomes an obstacle course. There are times when we get hit and fall again with more challenges and struggles. The easiest thing is to stop. But as a child learning to move, the more times we get up after falling, the stronger we become.

# 21

## FROM ANGER—
## TO MOTORCYCLES

The road to recovery began with a 1981 R65 BMW motorcycle. We had a friend in Chicago who owned a dealership. It didn't take much convincing with the husband to purchase a motorcycle since he had previously owned one. My new bike was red, very well balanced, and the perfect bike to learn on.

The most challenging part was wearing the helmet. I got a full-face helmet for safety reasons. (Okay, well, cosmetic reasons too. I spent too much money on skin care to end up with permanent road burn on my face.) It wasn't long until I discovered just how claustrophobic I was. That helmet smothered me. Fortunately, I worked for a guy who had become like a brother to me. He was one hundred percent involved in the healing process.

Each day our sales team had an hour- long training session in the office. He was determined to get me past choking each time I put the helmet on. So, there I sat.... every day.... for an hour.... in that helmet. You can only imagine how attractive that looked with my business clothes. My co-workers were like a close- knit family so they quickly became my "support group" to get rolling on that bike. Not only did those training sessions serve as a tool for me to adapt to the helmet, they also served as an opportunity to teach lessons of overcoming obstacles and moving forward. If you face your fears intentionally each day, soon they are no longer fears.

Each person I worked with was understanding and encouraging. Just months before we had sat in that same training room celebrating the fact that I was carrying Isaac with an "I'm Pregnant Again" party. Now I sat there in a business dress and a motorcycle helmet. The unity and support had not changed, only the circumstances.

We lived a couple of blocks from the office so the husband, who worked with us at the time, would ride my beemer to work with me on the back. Breaks were spent in the parking lot playing on the bike. I will never forget the first time I soloed around the building (with my helmet on.) I was greeted with a round of cheers from co-workers as I turned the corner. I know this seems strange and insignificant but inside I felt I had reentered the land of the living.

# 22

## RIDING THROUGH CURVES— LEARNING TO LIVE WITHOUT HIM

R iding became therapeutic. We had six to eight close friends that were our constant riding companions. Most people think of support groups as attending meetings. There are numerous varieties of support groups. Mine just happened to be on two wheels.

A couple years had gone by since we said good bye to our little Isaac. I had enveloped myself in my career and received several promotions. Our marriage was still okay. Not much had changed. Any resentful feelings I had inside me toward Randall had disappeared completely.

He loved soldiers and the military from the time he was a small child. He had been involved with a Civil War Reenacting group for quite a while. However, we were not prepared when he came home one afternoon, during the middle of his junior year, and said he needed his father's signature to go to Fort Benning for basic training the following summer. WHAT?? Sure enough, he had been speaking with a recruiter for the Ohio National Guard and wanted to spend his summer at Fort Benning. He was only seventeen so he needed a parent's signature to go.

That summer felt like hell from two perspectives. We were not allowed to communicate with him at all. Occasionally, he would be allowed to call home for a very few minutes. Other than that, we were completely cut off. We had no idea what he was going through.

We heard of two boys dying from heat exhaustion that summer. So, it felt hellish from *our* perspective of having no communication. It felt hellish from *his* perspective as each time he called he would say, "It is as hot as hell down here."

His absence that summer left lots of time for long motorcycle rides. I began noticing that simple practical things would teach me life lessons. As was the case one day as I was riding my motorcycle through some curvy mountain roads. Since I had laid the bike down in a curve a few months prior, I was fearful when I would head into a sharp curve. Instead of taking the curve smoothly, I would tense up. That day as I rode through the curves of a winding mountainous road, this life lesson came to me. *When we face a challenge or difficulty we can use the same principles of riding a motorcycle through a curve to deal with it.*

The correct way to take a curve on a motorcycle is to down shift just before the curve, check the road for any obstacles, look past the curve, give it some gas and just let the bike move smoothly through.

When I would tense up at the head of a curve, sometimes I would forget to downshift. That would result in not having enough power to get through the curve. Other times I wouldn't look through the curve. Instead, I would focus on every single inch of the road along the way. That was when I would start to lose my balance. Let me share with you what I learned in those curves.

*Downshift* – Once the curve (or situation) is in sight, we need to downshift. We can do this by simply praying. God already knows what is on the other side of our situation. We just need to talk to him and ask his help getting us through to the place where the road is smooth and straight again. By downshifting, it slows the bike down to the point that you can regain the power it takes to make it completely through the curve. By praying, it slows us down long enough to seek God's direction, and gain His power moving forward. If we don't downshift, especially in a steep switchback curve, there just will not be enough power to move through it. Shifting gears in the middle of a curve can throw the bike. That is just like prayer. If we don't slow down and take the time to pray when we first face a challenge, we may not have what it takes to move forward.

*Obstacles* - When we check the road for obstacles, we then know what we are going to have to avoid. Many times, when we are faced with a challenge there may be something, or someone, that we should avoid all together. If we were to connect with that obstacle in the road, it could cause the bike to wreck and even be fatal to us. Obstacles, in life's situations, come in many shapes and sizes. Some could be well meaning people yet they could slow us down to the point that we can't get through our curve or situation. Other obstacles could be activities that steal our time and prevent us from focusing on the situation. When going through a curve, stay away from anything blocking the road.

*Look Past the Curve* - Looking past the curve was the one I had the most difficulty with. When you are riding a motorcycle the bike WILL go where you are looking. If you are looking to the side of the road you WILL drift in that direction. When we are facing a challenge in life, the most important thing is to remain focused on where you want to end up. What you want your result to be. I can't emphasize enough what a difference that makes. When we are in the middle of a difficulty in life, it is SO easy to be overwhelmed with every single detail along the way. We seem to continually repeat those details in our mind and they usually make their way out of our mouths. That is when and where our emotions get so twisted. When riding a bike, we can become more concerned about the small drop off on the edge of the pavement than the smooth straight road ahead of us. When we focus too much on that drop off, we ride right toward it. If we keep our eyes on the place where we want to end up, the bike WILL go that way. Our life will do the same if we stay focused on our hopes and dreams instead of our challenges.

*Give It Some Gas* – This is easy but it involves removing fear and being intentional. When you are riding a motorcycle, and see the straight road at the end of the curve, you must give that bike some gas. If not, you will lose your balance and topple over. This is the easiest yet most important part of getting through the curve. Same with life. Just seeing the smooth path at the end of our situation will accomplish nothing unless we are intentional in moving toward it. One of the most powerful verses in the Bible says that knowing to do something and not doing it, is a sin. Just because we have a dream for something doesn't mean we will get there. It's like planning a trip. We can make all the travel plans in the world, but unless we intentionally get in a car, on a plane or a ship and move toward it, we will never see the destination.

*Move Smoothly* – A motorcycle can be one of the smoothest moving vehicles with the right momentum. If we have prayed at the beginning of a situation instead of trying to handle it all ourselves…. checked the circumstances for any obstacles we need to avoid…. identified the place where we are going…. Then, God will take us through that curve with what can seem like effortless smooth motion. Enjoy the ride!

That lesson kept me focused on Randall coming home at the end of that summer instead of the daily emptiness in the house.

He completed the first part of basic training between his junior and senior year. After graduating from High School the next spring, he returned to Fort Benning for Advanced Infantry Training. My boy was all grown up. The second summer of being separated from him wasn't as hard as the first year but it was by no means easy. We were beginning to learn to live without him.

His independence was that of a typical eighteen- year old. He was still very respectful yet loved making his own decisions. I was fortunate that he would still include me in his plans with his friends. Weekends sometimes found us at the bowling alley at midnight for black light "cosmic" bowling. As Y2K drew near for the passage from 1999 to 2000, we learned that he was not going to be able to attend our family Christmas in Tennessee. Since moving to Ohio, we had only missed one family Christmas there. The Ohio National Guard, with which he was now very active, could not be more than one hour away from their Armory from Dec 1, 1999 to Jan 31, 2000. The anxiety was that computers may fail to make the conversion from 1999 to 2000. If that were the case, the

National Guard had to be ready to step in within any given hour to control the chaos.

He asked if he could go to Tennessee for a few weeks during October to spend time with family. How could we say no? After all, he would be twenty years old within a few weeks.

# 23

## PERFECTLY NORMAL—
## A RESPONSIBLE NINETEEN-YEAR OLD

The day Randall left for Tennessee was as normal as any other time he was leaving to go on a trip. He came down the stairs carrying absolutely as much stuff as he possibly could to avoid making another trip from his room to his truck. It was a very common sight to see him looking like a pack mule on a narrow path as he made his way down the steps. Remember he was a civil war reenactor. He could leave for a reenactment weekend with the entire camping site in his arms and his rifle slung over his shoulder.

There was a small landing about ¾ of the way down the stairs. On this landing, you would turn to the right to continue down a few more steps into the living room. Randall's rifle was always slinging as he made the turn. That landing was the home of my large ceramic Tiger we had named "Elmer". Apparently one day, while I was in the hospital with Isaac, the rifle took out the side of Elmer's head. He had been strategically positioned so, after I came home from the hospital, it took me weeks to notice. Randall was probably thinking that I had enough going on with the baby. Why bother me with the fact that he had taken out Elmer's head? Regardless of the number of times he had been warned to be careful making that turn.

After packing his truck the day he left for Tennessee, he came back in the kitchen to kiss me goodbye. I remember watching him walk back to the truck and having a sick feeling in my stomach. I could only connect it with the days we said goodbye to him knowing he was going to basic training. I never mentioned it and thought I was only having a protective moment. We had spoken to him a few times after he arrived in Tennessee. After living through the two summers with him in Fort Benning, we were just happy knowing we could reach him any time we wanted.

Randall had two brothers and a sister from his mom's previous marriage. During this visit, he was staying with one of the brothers and his family. He had always idolized this brother and wanted to follow in his footsteps. We knew he was perfectly content to be where his brother was so we were happy knowing he was getting time with family. He was busy making those rounds. He had a girlfriend who had gone to Texas for college. He decided to fly there to see her before he came back to Ohio. He called and told us he was getting a side job with his brother's employer to earn the money for a plane ticket. It seemed perfectly normal. Randall was very responsible.

That employer was constructing a building with the intention of leasing it out. Randall was hired to help with this project. We knew he didn't have any construction experience, but we weren't exactly sure what all he had learned at basic training. We knew his work ethic, and we knew that employer was getting a bargain for $6 an hour. Since it was only a side job for a short- term goal we didn't doubt his decision.

# 24

## JUMPED IN THE CONVERTIBLE— AND TOOK OFF

October 11, 1999 was a normal Monday morning. I was playing in my ladies' tennis league at the tennis center in Cincinnati. As usual after the match we sat around chatting before showering and dressing for the day. The husband and I were working at the same location in Cincinnati. We never rode to work together. Most of the time he would ride his motorcycle and open the business and I would make it in around noon and close it at night. I had left the tennis center and was making my way to the office.

On that Monday, as I was traveling down the interstate from the tennis center, I got a call from my mom in Tennessee. I was in my little red Mazda RX7 two seat convertible with the top down. I could barely hear what she was saying because of the wind. I did hear that Randall's brother had called her and told her that Randall had been in a work accident. They were taking him to a small local hospital. She was on her way and would call me as soon as she knew more. Within a short time, I arrived at the office and was telling his dad about the accident. We had no details at all and could not reach any family members. My mom had stopped at Randall's grandmother's house on her way to the hospital to let her know what was going on. While there, she received a call saying that he was being transported to the trauma unit at the University of Tennessee Medical Center.

After the update call from mom I looked at his father and said, "We've got to leave for Knoxville right now. This can't be good." All we knew at this point was that he had fallen. I grabbed my purse and he grabbed his sunglasses and we jumped in the convertible and took off. Our home was in Dayton which was about an hour north. We could not waste any time taking the bike home and switching cars to make the trip in the SUV. The convertible was my fun run around car. It was a 1989 model and had well over 100k miles on it. All we were concerned about was getting to Knoxville.

We were speeding every chance we could while driving down I-75 South. Even though we had made that trip numerous times since we had lived in Ohio, nothing looked familiar as we sped down the interstate. We still could not get any information from family. I had called mom and told her we were on our way and she reminded me that cell signals in the hospitals were bad and sometimes not permitted. We knew nothing except our son was in trouble. At one point along the way we were pulled over for doing over 100 miles an hour. After explaining to the cop, he gave us an escort to the next county and told us to slow down.

We could not get any of our family to answer their phones. We know now they were using the fact that they were in the hospital with bad signal as an excuse to not pass information to us. During the drive our emotions were like a pinball in a pinball machine. They were all over the place and could completely change directions in a second only to change again a few seconds later. One minute we were convinced he was okay and only taken to UT as a precaution. The next minute we had convinced ourselves that he was dead and no one wanted to tell us. A second later we had convinced ourselves that he was probably hurt and would need a long recovery then we would begin to make plans for his long-term care. Within another minute, we were back to believing he was still okay and only taken to UT as a precaution.

Three hours after we left, we arrived at parking garage at the University of Tennessee Medical Center. We were immediately directed to the elevators leading to the trauma floor. When we stepped through the elevator doors we saw the faces of every family member. It had been years since some of them had even been in the same room with each other. That in and of itself was weird. As I glared around the room I also saw the faces of some of our very best friends from our hometown. I saw my mom sitting on a sofa with someone beside her that I did not recognize.

Before we arrived at the hospital we had made the decision that we were not going to talk to anyone until we had a chance to see Randall and talk with the doctor.

As we began to walk through the crowded waiting room I felt the uncomfortableness and awkwardness of no one knowing what to say to us. I had quietly asked my mom who the man was sitting with her. She told me it was the chaplain. (I guess it made sense that a chaplain was there. After all we were in the trauma unit.) The husband had politely told everyone that we loved them but wanted to see Randall and talk to the doctor first. The nurse immediately ushered us to his room and said the doctor would be right in. As we were walking to his room I overheard the husband's brother say, "Has anyone told them yet?" Told us WHAT? No one was telling us ANYTHING!

My heart sank as we peeped into Randall's room. There he lay with his head all wrapped in a white bandage and hooked up to several machines. As we moved closer we felt of his arm. He was warm. He had a pulse. The machines showed vitals. The doctor walked in right behind us and shut the door. He was very kind but told us in all his years of trauma care he had never seen anyone survive the severe head injury Randall had. What did that mean? Our only remaining son was going to die? Surely, he was exaggerating and meant Randall would need long term care. NO, that is not what he meant at all. He told us to begin saying our goodbyes. By all standards, Randall was brain dead.

We learned that the employer had placed him on a steel beam twenty feet above a concrete slab doing sheet roofing. Not only did Randall not have any experience in sheet roofing he was not even given a hard hat or any form of cable for protection. He had lost his balance and had fallen on his head.

The doctor explained that the head trauma had caused his brain to swell and there was basically no brain activity. The body was still reacting with a small amount of gag reflex but that would not last very much longer. That was impossible. I could see for myself that he was just sleeping. His body was warm to the touch. He had a heartbeat. Maybe the doctor had overreacted? We could see he would, no doubt, need long term care but he would surely wake up from this coma state he was in!

We could only stand in shock and look at each other. Could this be happening to us AGAIN?

Complete shock had set in. As we walked back to the waiting room most of our family and friends were crying and wanting to give us a hug. I could not shed the first tear. I was receptive to the hugs but basically was just staring into space. This had to be a dream. Family that normally would not be anywhere near each other were together in one place. The friends that were the dearest to us, that did not even know each other, were all gathered close. We were being told our nineteen- year old son was not going to live. I had to be having a nightmare. I just needed to somehow wake up!

I made my way to mom and asked her why the chaplain had left. She then shared with me that she had only told me that to protect me from the moment. The man that had been sitting beside her was with the organ donors. WHAT? They were there waiting before the child's parents were even informed of the situation? DAMN VULTURES!

Friends in Ohio were waiting for our call. In the mix of trying to process and communicate the facts we had just heard, we needed to arrange some things due to our sudden departure. We had to have a friend take the motorcycle back to our home and go in and shut the windows we had left open. We were also realizing we were going to be staying there for an undetermined amount of time and all we had with us was the clothes on our back.

Our pastor was once again an amazing comfort dealing with yet another tragedy in our lives. The word spread quickly through our church in Ohio. Within an hour or so of our phone call, we were told that three men were driving down with an RV to park in the parking lot at the hospital. It would be there for our comfort the entire time we were there with Randall. Some of the ladies called and asked for a list of what we needed from our home so they could send it down with the men. During our time of shock, people were stepping up to handle the practical needs we had. That right there is true Christianity and true examples of "God's people".

We were going to be spending the night and God only knew how much longer in the hospital. One of our friends went shopping and bought us comfortable sweats to wear while we waited. The husband was wearing his contacts but did not have his eyeglasses with him. He had to make a short trip out to a quick stop optometrist to get a pair of glasses made. That was Monday night. Of course, there was no sleeping. Only two people were allowed in Randall's room at a time. Even though his dad and I did not want to leave his side, we knew it was important for others to have their time with him as well.

Sometime during the early morning hours, I went back to his room. Randall's brother whom he had been staying with before the fall was standing alone beside his bed. My heart broke for him. Did he feel responsible? Did he think the family would blame him? During a shocking tragedy like that it is common to be numb to the feelings of others. Oftentimes, the first thing hurting people do is look to place blame. Sometimes it is toward other people and sometimes it is toward ourselves. I hadn't thought about how he must be feeling until I saw him standing there. I had to tell him I personally did not blame him. It was an accident. I pray to this day that deep down inside he has been released from any unwarranted quilt he may have walked away with.

# 25

## GAVE CONSENT—
## DEPOSITED ANOTHER
## TREASURE IN HEAVEN

The long night turned into two days. Who knew if the sun came up and went down? All we knew was that it was now Wednesday and all body reactions had ceased from our son. The machines were still doing their life appearance deception as we sat with him in his room. Randall was warm, his heart was beating and he looked only to be sleeping. But today I noticed grey matter coming from his ear. The nurses had done the final gag reflex test with no results. It was time for a decision. The unspoken question had haunted us for the past twelve hours. Do we have the machines turned off?

The decision became clearer for us when the doctor told us that Randall's death could have been pronounced when he was taken to the first local hospital. It had been reported to him by the staff that they had been instructed to keep him alive until his parents got there. That was when the decision was made to transport to UT Trauma. Even though we were faced with the same ending at least we had been given time by his side to process the tragic shock and say goodbye. We had the opportunity to embrace and be embraced by our family and friends as Randall's time on earth ended. We gave our consent to have the machines unplugged. On October 13, 1999, we deposited yet another treasure in heaven.

Sometime within those thirty- six hours the organ donor con-
sultants had managed to weasel their way back to us. Even though
the thought itself brought a sick feeling, we knew the right thing
to do was to offer life. How fortunate could a dying person be to
receive an organ from a healthy young man? But it was OUR young
man! But what if we were the parents waiting for an organ to save
our child instead of the ones deciding to give organs? Sometimes
you just do the right thing because it is the right thing to do. If
we had waited until our emotions and clear thoughts caught up
to the situation, it would have been too late for Randall's body to
offer life to anyone. One thing we did know was the heart of that
young man before he died. He was the most giving, kind, gener-
ous, forgiving, respectful young man anyone would have wanted
to know. We let that heart make the decision for us. What would
Randall tell us to do? There was only one answer when we looked
at it that way. Anything other than offering his organs to help save
a life would have been total selfishness on our part.

It was going to be a few hours while they harvested the organs
and before the funeral home came for his body. There was no
reason to spend any more time in that waiting area. It was a sad
weepy time as family and friends who had been with us the entire
time began to leave. We hung back and waited until everyone left
to have some time alone before we went to our hometown and
began the process of making his funeral arrangements. Although,
our time alone basically consisted of just sitting and staring at each
other in disbelief.

We finally gathered our strength and made our way to the parking garage. My little red convertible had not been moved since we
parked it upon our arrival Monday afternoon. We got in, turned
the key. **BOOM**!!! I guess the motor had taken all it could with the
speed driving on the trip down. It had blown up as the husband
started the car. That was just a little more than we could take at
that moment. That was the hit that broke down what little strength
we had mustered up. There we both sat crying and trapped in the
parking garage with a car that would not start.

94

By then all our family had arrived back in our hometown which was about forty minutes away. My sister in law received our desperate call for help and graciously made the drive back to pick us up. In addition to making funeral arrangements for Randall, we had to deal with getting the car towed and repaired. I know that seems small in comparison to the three previous days at the hospital but when you are already at the edge of holding it together or completely losing it, it felt like we were standing on a cliff deciding if we should jump.

# 26

## FREEBIRD—
## BUT NOT THE 20 MINUTE
## VERSION

Once we arrived in our hometown, the informative calls began. So many people in so many places had been praying for us and were awaiting our phone calls. Our family and friends, even though they were in shock and hurting too, were offering to help. Many were suggesting we just lay down and rest while they take care of the initial phone calls. Even though the gesture was appreciated, there was no resting in sight. Our minds were racing faster than cognitive thoughts could keep up with. There were phone calls, funeral arrangements, we needed to buy clothes to wear and the car issue. What we wanted to do was crawl in a hole and wait for the nightmare to end.

There was a certain amount of awkwardness with the family because of divorces. Several people Randall loved had not spoken to each other in years. We were then making decisions on how to honor him and include everyone. Choices had to be made to put differences aside and honor a young man that everyone loved. I will say it all that went smoother than either the husband or I imagined it could have. Sometimes losing someone sheds light and puts perspective on life. I only wish Randall could have seen his entire family together in one place getting along before he went to Heaven.

The funeral home was run by a local family and sat on a hill above a train track. Being from such a small town, they had also taken care of other family members when they passed. The owners could not have been more accommodating.

Randall was so young. If he had lived two more weeks he would have turned twenty years old. He lived a very active life being involved in both the Ohio National Guard and his Civil War Reenactment Unit. His favorite band was without a doubt *Lynard Skynard*. *Star Trek* still held a special place in his life and his passion for trains was equally as strong as when he was ten. How could we bring all this together and honor him within a one hour time frame?

What do we bury him in? The army greens of the National Guard or the Civil War uniform he had sewn himself? Of course, Randall would be buried beside his mother! Who sings? Would our pastor from Ohio be willing to come to Tennessee to speak? The fog in our minds continued. By now family and friends had begun showing up in several places bringing food. We were greeted by people who were offering condolences at every family members' house. That is a sweet part of living in the South. People take care of their neighbors when a death occurs.

Making decisions and arrangements during a time of shock came easier than we anticipated. Both his National Guard Unit and his Civil War Unit made the decision to be with us for his funeral. One of our closest friends, Rich, who had gotten Randall involved in Civil War Reenactments was one of the first people to arrive from out of town. I will forever have an image etched in my brain of Rich sitting at mom's house in a rocking chair. It seemed to have been no time since we had left the hospital until Rich had driven down from Ohio and made himself available to us for whatever we needed. WOW! What a friend! Even though we had had many fun times together in Dayton and we loved him dearly, whenever I think of Rich I see him sitting in that rocking chair just being available to us for whatever. He instantly became and remains one of my favorite people. That could not have been easy for him because he loved our son and thought so highly of him.

You never know when just making yourself available can make a lasting impression.

Randall's National Guard Unit also informed us that they would be making the trip and would appreciate the opportunity to be involved in his funeral. Now we were looking at the timing for everything. Our Pastor and his precious wife had told us that whatever, whenever we decided, they would be there. That was Thursday. I think under normal protocol we should have had visitation on Friday and had his ceremony Friday night or Saturday. But we just didn't have it together emotionally or practically. Sunday would have been appropriate but why take Pastor away from the church family on Sunday when we could just as easily make it all happen on Monday. So, that is what we did. We kept Sunday evening for visitation and planned his ceremony for Monday afternoon.

We decided to bury him in the Civil War uniform he had sewn himself. Looking back, we have questioned that decision thinking he worked so hard for two summers to earn his Army greens and we could have kept the one he had made. But it was what it was, the clothing decision was made. I came a long way from not wanting to see my Daddy in a casket to saying our son looked awfully handsome.

What about *Lynard Skynard*? We had been communicating several times a day with our Pastor about the plans. We asked him what he thought of playing *"Freebird"*[1]. His immediate response was "YES, Absolutely, but let's not use the twenty- minute version". That was funny. Can you image a funeral with twenty minutes of *"Freebird"*?[2] Even though for time sake we didn't, Randall sure would have loved that. Not sure what to do about the trains. I guess that would have to remain a memory to cherish instead of working something into his ceremony.

Sunday afternoon we prepared ourselves and made our way to the funeral home to greet our friends and family who came to say goodbye. I remembered to wear comfortable shoes and it was a good thing. We could not see the end of the line of people for hours.

The National Guard Unit posted a soldier at one end of his casket and the Civil War Unit posted a soldier at the other end.

They would often change throughout the evening but there were always two soldiers guarding his casket. The funeral home was so accommodating that they had literally offered to let the reenactors set up a campsite in their yard. The soldiers opted for hotel rooms but the thought of a business going over and above to give the family whatever they needed to make a lasting memory of their loved one is usually unheard of in the society we live in today.

The husband and I had both grown up in the same small town. We had gone to two different high schools, had grown up in two different churches and yet attended a third one together before we were married. My family had always lived on the East side of town and his on the West. People we had connected with in our lives were literally coming from all directions for hours. We appreciated each hug we got and each tear we shed. There is no gesture too small when a family loses a child.

Monday afternoon came too soon. After a night of sympathetic people giving their condolences, it was time to give all the focus to Randall. We made our way to the funeral home early Monday afternoon. There was one last visitation prior to the ceremony for our friends arriving from Ohio. Hugs and tears from them were the prelude we needed to begin the ceremony. Everything went perfectly in order. Prayers, Hymns, *"Freebird"*[3] and *"Angel"*[4] by Sarah McLachlan. The Pastor stood to make his way to the podium as *"Angel"*[5] completed with the lyrics, *"You're in the arms of the angel, May you find some comfort here"*. There was a brief pause of silence as a train went through town on the tracks below the funeral home blowing its whistle. What timing! It could not have been planned and it could not have been more perfect! You could hear the sniffles and see the tears in the room go to a different level as that train went by. For those of us who deeply understood his love for trains we felt as if God was saying to us, "He is with me, I've got him and I've got you. Take comfort in that." He had put the final touch on the celebration of Randall's life that we could not have planned.

The graveside was less than a mile from the funeral home. A long- lived tradition in the South, which I love, is for a line of cars to follow the hearse from the funeral home to the graveside. Yes, and in the South, we still follow the courtesy of stopping and pulling to the side of the road when a funeral procession passes by. It just shows respect. Randall's funeral procession wasn't a long journey but it was a long procession filled with love to follow him on the last leg of this life on earth.

Once at the cemetery we took our place in the chairs provided for us beside the grave. It was a beautiful fall day with a crisp nip in the air. Trees were radiant with colors of yellow, orange and red. After a few words from the Pastor, bagpipes began playing *Amazing Grace*[6] in the distance. In my spirit, I could feel the presence of God all around. Yet, having become a Trekkie by osmosis during the marriage, in my head I could also hear the words of Captain Kirk at Spock's funeral as the bagpipes began to play *Amazing Grace*.[7] "Of all the souls, I have encountered in my travels, his was the most......human"[8]

As one final military recognition, there was a twenty- one gun salute. Half was done by the National Guard and their rifles. The other half was done by the Civil War Reenactors with their rifles, musket and black powder. A fitting ending to a life well lived.

# 27

## TENNESSEE—
## PLACE OF MY BIRTH,
## PLACE OF MY DEATH

One of the most surreal moments we had after Randall passed was when we found and read this poem he had written. Had we known, this *unedited* version would no doubt have been included in his funeral.

Tennessee oh Tennessee,
my home my birthplace,
Love of my life!
My mind dwells on you often,
your rivers run through my viens.
Your mountains grow ever more beautiful
in my mind.

How I love the smell of the blue rain
upon your wooded hills.
The sight of your fog rolling
like a blanket over your legs
Of ancient hills and mountains
wakes my spirit,
like the rain upon a tin roof.
Your lakes create paintings
on the canvas of my heart,
When kissed by a setting sun.

# RISE

Tennessee, place of my birth,
place of my death.
Place of mysteries
and of peace,
Place of death
and place of life.

Tennessee,
love of my life.

# 28

## NO TREE, NO TRAIN—
## BUT A BASKET OF LOVE

Everything had happened so fast the week Randall went to Heaven. We had the car towed and repaired with a new engine amidst making his final arrangements. Our heads were still spinning. What just happened? Is this real or were we continuing in a nightmare? How do we go back to Ohio without him? There was no such thing as normal in our lives. Before returning home and attempting a life without him, we took a few days and rented a cabin in the Smoky Mountains. I'm not sure exactly what we thought we would accomplish there but being alone without phones and the idea of not having to talk to anyone certainly appealed to us.

Arriving back in Ohio several days later was gut wrenching. How could we pull up to that condo and go into his room? It is one thing to be surrounded by family and friends during a crisis but it is something entirely different to go back into a condo where there used to be life and face the emptiness. Once again, our "God's person" and his wife were right by our sides. They met us at the condo when we arrived in Dayton and we all went inside together.

Randall lived a very systematic, well organized life and things were done very methodically. His room was like a Civil War museum. When I would go in to dust and clean his room, if I placed something back just a half inch from where it was originally sitting, he would notice it as soon as he walked in and gently move it right back into its original position. The thought of walking into that room where he had everything perfectly placed left a pit in my stomach that felt like lead.

As I sat on his bed and looked around the room, memories flooded my mind, tears rushed down my cheeks but giggles made their way into my voice as I thought of our Confederate Flag struggle. When he became a reenactor, he decided that the Confederate Flag would make a nice curtain for the one window in his bedroom which faced the front of our condo. I went to the mailbox one morning and looked up. Keep in mind, all the condos looked the same which made his one window scream with red, white and blue. His Southern pride never gave in to the fact that we lived in Ohio and neighbors may be offended. For days, I would take it down and put the curtains back up only to find the flag back in the window the following day. We eventually met a compromise of using the flag as a bed cover so it was prominently on display as one entered his room.

His room was now vacant and I could sleep there instead of sleeping on the sofa. That just wasn't right! I couldn't make that my bedroom. I'd never get any sleep. I know there are several studies that say never make a major decision the first year after a major tragedy. Well, there are always exceptions. We began looking for a house. How could we continue to live in that condo when we saw Randall around each corner? I would forever be looking for his truck to pull into the driveway.

One of the saddest days was when two of the soldiers from his National Guard unit came to gather his issued belongings. These soldiers were children themselves and they cried as they were gathering his gear. They kept apologizing for the tears and said that was the first time they had done a task like that. I could tell they were trying to be strong but it did us all good that day to have a long cry.

Our church in Ohio had planned a memorial service for him for the members who were unable to attend his funeral in Tennessee. It was such a sweet ceremony and such a blessing to hear the teenagers and youth Pastor talk and share their memories of Randall.

In true teenage fashion their views were sometimes quite comical. One of the girls talked about his hair before he went to basic training. Prior to the military, she said he had the *Frisch's* or *Shoney's Big Boy* haircut. We had never thought about it....... but it was true. The laughter and hugs from our Ohio *"framily"* was exactly what we needed to begin to make the transition into our new life without him.

We found a house that suited us well. It was in a little quaint town called Waynesville between Dayton and Cincinnati. We had a two-acre beautiful four season yard. We both fell in love with the house for our own reasons. The husband/ photographer loved the fact that it had a built in dark room on the lower level. (If you don't know what a dark room is, just do research on photography history) I, on the other hand, was ready to sign the papers when I saw the 11x11 closet. The house became therapy to occupy our minds or at least find a new way to numb the surmounting pain we continued to carry inside.

We bought the house and moved by the end of November. The outpouring of love we were still receiving was amazing. A long driveway lined with Bradford Pear trees was a beautiful guide from the street to the house. Each day I walked to the end of the driveway, looked in the mailbox, and was greeted with cards coming from our friends throughout the United States. We had peers and co-workers from all over North America reach out as the word was beginning to spread about Randall. We were blessed to have received such warm expressions of love for an extended time. I remember, however. the day I walked down the driveway to the mailbox, looked inside, and it was empty. I wasn't feeling any pity for myself but I did feel all alone for the first time since his accident. Standing there, staring into an empty mailbox signaled the time had come to rebuild life and it was up to me to move forward.

Maybe the cards in the mailbox had stopped but the waves of love had not. On the morning of Dec. 1, 1999 I got a call from my dear friend, Cindy asking if she could stop by the house for a minute. When she arrived, she was carrying a large basket full of beautifully wrapped small presents. As we sat in the great room with a cup of coffee, she explained that one present was to be opened each day from Dec. 1 to Dec. 25. Twenty- five families from our church had gotten us a small present and placed a note of encouragement in it.

The first year after losing someone is the hardest. Each changing season, each holiday, each special day (such as a birthday) brings bittersweet memories. Christmas season 1999 was the worst. Christmas had always been Randall's favorite holiday. Up until the 1999 season, Christmas presents had to be strategically placed around the train track wrapping itself underneath the tree. The whistles and chugging of the train going in continuous circles had become an intimate sound of Christmas in our home. But this year there was no tree, there was no train, there was no Randall.

Each day we looked forward to opening our present from the basket. None of the gifts were expensive yet they were priceless to us. We received everything from candles, candy, small plaques, homemade gifts and goodies to books. With each gift, there was a hand- written note of encouragement. Some were scriptures, some were poems, some were cards with a loving note and some of our closest friends included things that they knew would make us laugh. That was our basket of love!! No matter where I live or where this life takes me, I will always have that basket with me and the memories of the love it contained.

# 29

## BEST OF INTENTIONS—
## STILL CUT DEEP

I understand from the perspective of a person doing their best to relate to a grieving family they often don't know what to say. Amidst all the expressions of sincere love there were also things said that cut deep or left us shaking our heads. I don't include these in any way meaning to sound unappreciative of anyone's sincere attempts to console. I only want to share from someone on the receiving end of those sincere, yet unnerving, gestures in hopes to make others more aware and sensitive when talking with hurting people.

I learned that some things said were indeed just old traditional sayings that had no truth to them. For example, when the babies passed, you would not believe how many times we heard, "Well God just needed another angel." Other things said were "Another flower was just planted in God's garden," "It's all for the best," or "I'm sure losing Randall was harder on you than losing the babies", and even "God lost His son too." However, I think the most damaging was from a speaker giving the testimony of her daughter living through a tragic accident. It was very strongly implied that the amount of faith she had was what kept her daughter alive. If that were true, then the opposite of that must be true as well. Our lack of faith is why our Randall passed.

Let's take a quick look at each one of these.

*"God just needed another angel."* With all the sincerity and kindness in my heart I know people see their children that have

passed as little angels. It is a sweet thought of our babies pictured as innocent little angels with wings. They are indeed precious but they are not angels. God created angels before humans THEN He created humans in HIS image. I didn't write the Bible so please feel free to search this for yourselves. It appears to me that while we are here on the earth we are indeed a little lower than the angels. If you believe Jesus was God's son and became human, then let's look at what that means. If you don't want to have this discussion just jump on over to the next chapter.

It tells us in Hebrews that when Jesus became human He became a little lower than the angels. Hebrews 2:7 AMP "You made Him for a little while lower {in status} than the angels; You have crowned Him with glory and honor, and set Him over works of your hands; You have put all things in subjection under His feet {confirming his supremacy}." That having been said, I believe that as humans on this earth we can agree that we have a little lower rank than the angels. But let's look at what happens next.

We get a glimpse into heaven in 1 Cor. 6:3. NIV "Do you not know that we are to judge angels? How much more, the things of this life!" I'll admit I don't know what all that is going to look like but obviously, we can't judge angels that we can't see on this earth. It appears to me that those who believe and become children of God will one day be in a place of judging the angels. Therefore, while we are on the earth as humans, we are lower than the angels. However, for those of us who believe and go to Heaven we seem to blow right past the angels into a position higher than them.

Whatever your interpretation is, it seems clear to me that no humans, at any time, grow wings and become little angels. We will talk more about our babies in eternity later. But for now, let's just entertain the thought that while it is a sweet precious image to hold onto, our babies who now live in heaven rank much higher than an angel. They are 100% perfect, healthy and happy. They never face any evil or deal with any pain. Even the ones we never saw because of abortion or very early miscarriage, we will recognize and know them immediately as our own.

*"Another flower was just planted in God's garden."* Wow, this one still leaves me shaking my head. It was not said to me directly but to a dear friend of mine when his baby son went to heaven. He sarcastically told me, "Yep, apparently, there is a garden somewhere made up of kids." I asked around and was told that maybe somewhere years ago, there was an old song with lyrics referencing that. After researching, the only thing I could find was a children's song about being the flowers in God's garden. The song referenced international children and how the variety of skin colors makes a beautiful garden. This should not be taken out of context by saying that a baby who has passed was just planted in God's garden. I am sure this was said by someone out of nervousness or being at a loss for words. However, I can assure you that a baby created in God's image does not automatically turn into a plant and sprout petals around their face like a flower. Even though this was most likely said with compassion, it still cuts deep to the hurting parent. They just had to give up their own flesh and blood and now that child is being referenced as a plant? Not only does this belittle the child but it plants seeds or reinforces the lie that God was the one taking that child for a better cause, which leads me into the next one.

*"It's all for the best"*. NO, IT'S NOT!! The best would be if there were no sickness, disease, pain, death, disappointment or tragedies on this earth. But there are and while we live on this planet, each day will be filled with different levels of pain and challenges. It is unavoidable. Did God cause these children to die? I can tell you that God is NOT the source of any of this pain. He can however take anything that comes into our lives and use it for our good. He does that differently for each person. No matter how you are feeling right now, just know that He is indeed for you and not against you, no matter what you have faced.

*"I'm sure losing Randall was harder on you than losing the babies."* Again, I have no doubt that when this was said, the person was sincerely trying to console. However, from my perspective, just the opposite was true. I was forced to take such a deep look at my belief about eternity with Stefan, Ephraim and Isaac. When Randall joined them my vision of Heaven and eternity was solid.

I saw it as a real place with real people. Heaven had become so real to me that my first reaction to someone passing had become jealousy. I know that may sound weird but it is true. There comes a point after so many losses and deposits into heaven that you begin to feel you have more there than you do on earth. I loved each one of the boys equally. I was fortunate to share earth time with Randall. I knew him. I knew his personality. I have memories of him that will forever remain in my heart. I have pictures of times we shared together. I know exactly what to expect when I see him again in Heaven.

The babies…not so much. I only have a heart full of unanswered questions. What would they have looked like? What would their personalities have been like? What would their interest on earth have been? What would their giggles have sounded like? One day all these questions will be answered but for now I can only speculate. From a mothers' heart, I believe Stefan would have been smart and athletic with a great sense of humor like my Dad. I believe Ephraim would have had much the same detailed introverted personality as his brother Randall and I believe Isaac would have been my little bundle of energy, laughter, and mischief. I feel certain he would have been a practical jokester like his mom and grandfather. One day I will know how close I came with my "guesstamations." But for now, the answers to these questions must wait.

So, for me, saying good bye, for now, to each child hurt in its own unique way. Who can measure or judge another person's pain? I had a connection with Randall I was not able to share with the babies. But how do you react when someone implies one hurt more than the others? One choice was to agree on the outside knowing on the inside it wasn't true. Another would be to contradict the statement which would have made the person trying to console me feel uncomfortable. I hope I politely said, "Each one hurt." Either way, statements like that leave the grieving person with no comfortable response.

"*God lost His son too.*" This one raises anger in me and the saddest thing is it was said by a pastor. There cannot even begin to be legitimate comparisons made here. It was just "religious" babble.

God GAVE his son. (The theology here is too deep to include but if it raises questions feel free to reach out to me on my website. www.Debralynnhayes.com) Just know that the first parents that ever existed also lost a child. Adam and Eve were faced with the tragedy of one child killing the other. There is no new pain under the sun. We can rest in the fact that we can take the smallest disappointment or the greatest tragedy to the Father in prayer and the Holy Spirit understands everything we feel and He will comfort us.

*"My lack of faith was the reason my children died"*. That is a lie straight from the pit of hell. I am sorry if I sound blunt and direct here but this one kept me questioning for years. I was already thinking that God had punished me for the abortion of Stefan with my other three sons dying. The last thing I needed planted in my head was that my faith or lack thereof had something to do with it too.

As I mentioned, it wasn't long after Randall died, when a lady come to our church as a guest speaker. We didn't question it because of the trust we had in our Pastor. I will admit too that we had such a raw wound going into the meeting that we took her words straight to heart. She told the story about her daughter's accident and how she was in a coma. With joy and zeal, she explained that after much prayer, her daughter recovered and was living a healthy normal life. Wow! That was an amazing testimony but when you are sitting there listening just a few weeks from standing at the grave of your son, it was hard to get excited with her. I admit my response was a sarcastic dry "Well Yeah for you!"

After the husband and I left the meeting our conversation was anything but positive. What is wrong with us that God didn't heal Randall? If OUR prayers weren't enough what about all the other people who prayed with us? We would never have enough faith for anything because nothing else would compare with importance. Deeper and deeper we dug into our melancholy worthlessness. A certain spiritual inferiority set in. She was favored by God and we were low lives. We decided we would not attend any further meetings with her.

I honestly say with all the kindness in my heart that I am thankful and happy for her that her daughter lived and that they are enjoying their earth time together. I am thankful she didn't have to live through the hell we did. I can honestly say too that our faith or lack thereof is not what put Randall in his grave. If we want to measure faith, I believe it takes much more faith to continue believing God is good when circumstances do not turn out as you would have wanted them to. We should never compare our circumstances to someone else, good or bad. Each one of us can have a personal relationship with God and He can help us through anything. Even on the days when we act as if we really don't want Him involved, He still has our backs and doesn't turn His back on us.

# 30

## JUSTICE OR INJUSTICE SYSTEM?— WHAT A DISGRACE

Our life in Ohio had become a life we never anticipated. Our dreams of a house full of children had been crushed. Once the shock began to wear off, the reality rushed in. Not only had the generation of our children been cut off but so had the next generation of our grandchildren. We were no longer parents and we would never be grandparents. The neglect of one man changed our future forever. That was hard to swallow.

We hadn't got Randall's body in the ground before we began receiving medical bills upon medical bills. Ambulance bills, hospital bills, doctor bills not to mention funeral cost. Should we be responsible for these? We took the bills to a lawyer and the law suit from hell was on.

It continued for three exhausting years. Our emotions were already drained and we had to keep the whole accident fresh in our minds daily until it was resolved.

Once the case was presented, the lies began. Keep in mind the man responsible for Randall's death had a large umbrella of insurance covering. Nothing we received from his insurance would have changed his life. We felt he should be held accountable for his neglect. He responded to his attorney with entirely different information.

The truth was, Randall was hired to help construct a building on personal property. The building was being built with the intention of being leased out when it was completed. There were no W-4 new employee forms signed. Randall received one pay check before his fall which was written from the employer's personal checking account.

The employer replied to his lawyer saying Randall was an employee of his business which was a hauling company. He and his attorney fought for Randall's death being filed under his Workman's Comp instead of negligence on his part. Workman's Comp was cut and dry with bills. Our negligence case took into consideration the unnecessary life changing loss we had experienced due to one person's careless actions. This fight continued for three years. Throughout the fight our attorney acquired tax records, business records and proof that Randall was doing work on personal property with no ties to the hauling business when he fell.

Hearing after hearing had been rescheduled. The day to appear before the judge arrived. We drove to Tennessee to meet with the lawyers and the judge. Sadly, it was treated no differently than a minor traffic violation.

Both sides presented their case and the judge deliberated for a while. He looked straight at us. With a solemn dry look on his face, he said we had presented everything we needed to prove to win the case. HOWEVER, to prevent future cases of employees suing their employers he was not going to be the judge that put that precedent on the books. We were encouraged to appeal it to a higher court.

ARE YOU KIDDING ME??? I could not believe what I was hearing. We won but the judge would not rule. Before I could stop my tongue, I yelled, "You Bastard!! Our child died because this man was too lazy and cheap to protect him. We are not talking about a broken arm here." I was gently escorted out of the courtroom but at least I wasn't escorted to jail for that outburst. No one will ever be able to convince me there was not some money or favors exchanged for that lack of ruling.

Once again, we found ourselves just starring at each other in disbelief. We were told it would be $4000 to take it to a higher court. Quite honestly, we were spent and I don't mean money. Our emotions had been ripped and torn for thirty- six months. We did not have it inside us to continue reliving the details of that fatal day. We settled to get the medical bills paid to the establishments who were willing to wait until our fight was complete. We then put an end to our nightmare and the employer got a few small fines from OSHEA.

It is a shame that our injustice system can put a price tag on a life taken by negligence then covered up by lies. Tears of sadness and anger flowed for the way he was disgraced by the employer responsible for his death. It showed the greed inside that man's heart by continuing to put the almighty dollar above truth and life.

There comes a point in time when you must make a conscious choice to lay down resentment, bitterness and anger. It will eat you up from the inside out and literally mess with your head. Trying to make sense of some situations is futile.

Approximately seven years from the time that Randall fell I was on a business trip in Boise, Idaho. Some moments are snapshots of life that never fade. I will never forget exactly where I was standing in the room and what I was wearing when the phone call came. A family member was asking me if I had heard any news from home. I had not. I ask why. They informed me that the man who was responsible for Randall's death had been murdered the night before. Without hesitation, my response was, "I didn't do it, I was out of state and I have alibis." My quick response certainly revealed that I hadn't given a lot of thought to forgiving.

The man had in fact been murdered in a shocking tragedy that made *USA Today Newspaper*. I quickly hung up the phone and found the national paper. Sure enough, there it was in a bold headline. The article stated that a family custody dispute had turned violent and three people were killed as their grandchild played ball. I was speechless. My emotions took a roller coaster ride inside my head with several ups and downs, twist and turns. Not that any reaction was required from me but seriously, how did I feel about this?

Admittedly my first knee jerk reaction was he got what he deserved. But as I dug into the article and received more phone calls from home relaying the news, I knew I could not leave this self- proclaimed justification in my head. When I spoke to the husband (who was an ex by that time) we threw around our own religious babble by making remarks like maybe that is what the Bible means when we read about vengeance belonging to the Lord.

NO! I could not let my emotions and feelings continue to get tangled in that web inside my head. This is what I referred to earlier when I said there comes a point when you just make a conscience choice to lay something down. When I looked at the whole scenario my heart broke for that child who was playing ball. He was approximately the same age as Randall was when I met him. That innocent child witnessed the violent killings of three of his grandparents at the same time. How could I allow myself to feel any justification about that? The God I serve would not get back at one man with the pain it caused to that child. That's when I made my choice to lay it down. There are just no answers to the pain and evil on this earth. Trying to pinpoint a proper reaction to that tragedy was destined to torment me.

God is not a God of confusion, so when confusion reigns high in my mind I search the Scriptures to find my clarity. When I land on the perfect verse for my situation there is a tremendous peace that follows. I didn't have to dig far to find my answer for this scenario. 1 Peter 5:7. Cast your cares. That scripture is quoted so often that sometimes I think we toss it around without a lot of thought. The word cast means to throw, hurl or fling. It doesn't mean to keep close in sight or thought. So, when I chose to let go of trying to make sense of the news of this man's murder I had to intentionally not dwell on it any longer. I love the way The Living Bible phrases this verse, "Let him have all your worries and cares, for he is always thinking about you and watching everything that concerns you." WOW everything means everything, big or small.

We need to get to the point where we realize we don't have to understand everything. There is a difference in casting and holding it all inside.

I could choose to dwell on all the negative facts that took Randall from this earth or I could remember the love I shared with him and all the positive influence and impact he left behind.

He indeed left a legacy. That became very apparent by the Ohio National Guard Unit where he was active.

While the lawsuit had been ripping us apart, the Ohio National Guard had given Randall some amazing honors. Outside the Armory in Xenia, Ohio there was a tree planted in his honor with a marker memorializing him. I visit that tree yearly and have thoroughly enjoyed watching it grow. In addition to the tree, the Guard created an award they give to an outstanding Specialist with character traits that measure up to what Randall presented.

Tears of happiness and love flowed for the way he was remembered. The stories told us by adult men about what an outstanding young man we had raised left us speechless and filled with gratitude.

# 31

## WHO I NEEDED— EXACTLY WHEN I NEEDED HIM

Sometimes God has a way of being a few steps ahead of you. Image that! My heart was exhausted with children. I could endure being around them for short periods of time but there was absolutely no way I was letting my heart get attached to a child again.

My first cousin, Jeff, who lived in Tennessee, and his wife Tesha were expecting a child in Feb. 2000. I had not lived in Tennessee for over ten years. Even though we were together at family functions we were not extremely close at the time. However, I remained close to his mom, my aunt Wanda. She kept me informed of all the family interactions just as any good southern aunt would. She was looking forward to this baby as it would be her 3rd grandchild. There had only been four months between Randall's passing the baby's due date. On the afternoon of Feb 12 I got the phone call that the baby was on the way. A little girl with ribbons and bows was expected.

Midnight came and went and no baby girl was added to our family. It was now Feb 13, my birthday. Was this sweet, ironic, or a cruel joke that the new baby was going to be born on my birthday? At 12:47 am the baby was welcomed into our family. HE weighed six pounds, six ounces and was twenty and one eighth inches long. What a surprise to everyone. The bundle of joy was a BOY!! I was three hundred miles away but my phone rang no later than 1:30am asking when I would be able to come home to meet Lucas Allen Hinkle. Oh my, another baby boy!! My heart sank with dread and leaped with excitement at the same time.

I had determined I would be able to play with Lucas from time to time and maintain a long- distance relationship. This would prevent any deep attachment. The first few visits proved to follow this path. However, once he was beginning to interact, it was a lost cause. I loved this little boy as much as if I had given birth to him. We were connected on such a deep level there were no words to describe. Many months later, on one of my return trips to Tennessee, I walked in the door unannounced and that baby looked up at me and said "My Dabbie." That moment heart became mush.

God has a way of knowing exactly who you need and exactly when you need them. My choice would have been to never let my heart be that vulnerable again. That little blond headed blue eyed baby boy was not cooperating with that choice. His giggles and expressions kept squeezing my heart as I kept squeezing him. Over the years our relationship has grown and I love him as my own. He has grown from the waddling toddler to the smart mouth teenager.

I found myself at a crossroad when Lucas was born. I could have just as easily chosen to put that hedge up around my heart once again. Oh my...how much love I would have missed. I don't even want to think about the crust that would have grown around my heart toward children if Lucas hadn't come along exactly when he did. I chose to open my heart very deliberately to this baby. Don't resist something that has the potential to cause pain when it could be the very thing that offers life, hope and healing.

# 32

## EMPTY ARMS SYNDROME—
## IT IS REAL

February 2000 brought another addition. Our new house kept us busy while becoming a regular hang out for our friends. We lived in a three- story house on two acres. That dwelling was screaming for a dog to love. In addition to that *Empty Yard Syndrome*, I was dealing with a huge case of the *Empty Arms Syndrome*. There is a syndrome called *Empty Arm Syndrome*. Some people recognize it as being real. Others think it is imagined. I found it to be true. When women lose children their arms and heart ache for something to hold.

For my birthday, the husband went to different shelters looking for a dog. I had my heart set on a Cocker Spaniel since I had owned that breed prior to moving to Ohio. He, on the other hand, owned English Bulldogs. He called me at work and I could hear the sniffles in his voice. He had not found a Cocker Spaniel but he had found a bulldog. My perception of bulldogs was nothing more than an abundance of slobbers. I didn't want slimy salvia dripping around in my new home. Yet, it was so rare to find full a blooded English Bulldog at a shelter. The dog had been dropped off the night before by a single guy who traveled and was not able to give the attention needed. Reluctantly, I agreed to go visit the dog.

Once at the shelter, I learned the difference between English Bulldogs and Olde English Bulldogges. The latter had a dry mouth and no slobber. Within five minutes inside the *get acquainted* room,

Buster was on his way to his new home. He was a about a year old and a beautiful brindle color. The husband still wanted me to have my Cocker Spaniel so we continued to make stops at other shelters thinking we would take home two dogs.

Buster lay quietly stretched out on the back seat chewing his new toy. As we made stop after stop looking for another dog we could hear him sighing deeply as if he was saying, "Am I not enough?" He indeed was enough so we took our new "baby" to his new home. Over the years, he proved to be the most sensitive dog I have ever known.

Buster was such a God sent. I had grown so attached to him that we discussed getting a female bulldog and naming her Maggie. One of our favorite friends from Tennessee had come up for a visit the following February. I was working a trade show at the local mall so during a break I wandered into the pet store. There she stood inside her little cage, fawn and white with big brown eyes, watching every move I made. I could tell by her long legs that she was also an Olde English Bulldogge.

My immediate phone call home was answered by our friend. I asked him to tell the husband that I had found Maggie and they needed to come to the mall. By the way, grab the checkbook. We hung up and the conversation between them sounded something like this: "Who is Maggie? Why is she lost? Evidently we need to pick her up at the mall and Deb needs the checkbook." Shaking his head, the husband knew he would be coming back to the house with another bulldog.

My empty arms were beginning to fill. I had two fifty- five -pound fur babies in my arms and on my lap. Both were sweet but with totally different personalities. Buster would rather spend his time outside and would quickly disappear exploring. Maggie would rather be inside right under our feet. Buster loved to go "bye bye" in the car and Maggie loved to watch TV. The first time I took the two of them to Tennessee to visit, my family laughed as I unpacked. In my big *baby bag,* I had a long leash for Buster and video tapes for Maggie. Close friends in Ohio had taped the West Minster Dog Show for Maggie to have as she traveled. She seemed to identify the dogs on screen and they captivated her attention for hours. Sometimes she would get so excited she would dive at the screen to join in the action. Having two Olde English Bulldogges was like having a couple of toddlers that would never grow up.

So yes, from someone with an experience, *Empty Arm Syndrome* is real. No animal could ever replace a child but loving on those two fur babies sure filled a void left in my heart and my arms.

# 33

## GOD, I CAN'T TRUST
## MY HUSBAND—
## I DON'T EVEN LIKE YOU

It was easy to fill my days with work, dogs, motorcycles, and an abundance of friends. However, late night and waking up early mornings were quite a different story. The alone time is the perfect place for thoughts to race. That is the most important time to take control of what you think.

The bedroom on the front of our house was a beautiful room with an attached glass solarium. I could sit comfortably under the glass in the sunshine, moonlight, storms, or snow experiencing the weather all around me. One night I was laying on the bed listening to a storm outside and letting my thoughts wander down a path of depression. The tears coming from my eyes were keeping pace with the rain running down the sides of the solarium. My thoughts of ending it all were illuminating my brain with the same force the lightning bolts were illuminating the yard. What did I really have to live for? All I could see was the death of my children, my failing marriage, and the uncertainty of my future. I lay there playing the reel over in my head of how I could check out. There were a couple paths I could take to go to sleep and never wake up.

No, they were not just passing thoughts. I felt all alone with no deep connection to anyone. The truth was there were lots of people in my life that loved me but my focus remained on what I had lost, not what I had. It is not uncommon to feel alone when your will is dying inside. Even though there may be people all around you.

We can take a quick look at Jesus and see this when he went into the garden before the cross. The emotions were different. He was not looking at ending it all. His battle of the will reflected his willingness to go through the pain of the cross. He could have taken any of his disciples with him yet he knew it was a place he had to go alone. By being alone he could not be distracted from the intensity of what had to be accomplished. His conversation with God was so deep he sweat drops of blood as he cried out for answers. He was human too. His burden was as heavy that night as ours will ever be.

God wants to bring us to that place with our own pain. However, we often choose to run away from the pain. We keep ourselves distracted by staying busy or staying surrounded by people. I admit, it is a scary place to think about going without the assurance of coming out of it better. It is especially a scary place to go when you already feel anger toward God. Only when we allow ourselves to feel the hurt on a deeper level can we gain the deeper healing we need. God isn't a fairy that will sprinkle fairy dust over our lives to make all the pain disappear and restoration begin. It is a process. I can guarantee you, you will not go through the process alone and you will discover love from God that you have never known.

As I lay on my bed alone that stormy night my choices were to end it or to pray. I knew deep inside that the only hope I had of letting go of those destructive thoughts was with God's help. I know, it seems weird, doesn't it? How can one think of God and suicide seconds apart? I'm sure it's more common than most people realize. Hopelessness latching onto thoughts is like tying a cement block to yourself and jumping into a body of water. That night I sat on that cliff inside my head for hours. Should I jump or should I pray?

The battle raged for hours. The darkness or the light? The angels or the demons? Life or death? Stay or go? When I got to that deep dark place it was literally... end or begin? I had reached the end of a road in my head. I could stop there, lay down, and die or I could look for a new path. But I could not return and keep reliving the tragedies I had been through.

I decided to say a prayer.

All I could get out of my mouth was this: "God I can't trust my husband and I don't even like you anymore." There I had said it. The raw thoughts were finally out of my mouth. I could not trust my husband and I really didn't think too highly of the identity that called himself God.

I know within a second of time it was the Holy Spirit that came right back in my thoughts with: "That's okay...all I need is faith the size of a mustard seed to completely heal you." I didn't audibly hear anything but the thoughts were as real and deep as if it had been a verbal response. A mustard seed huh? Even faith that small was a huge stretch for me. I honestly didn't think I could get anywhere near the size of a mustard seed with what was left of my faith. Nevertheless, I knew, with that response, that checking out of this life was not an option.

That was my first step toward my pain instead of away from it. I can honestly say that is where my healing began. Granted, the healing didn't come instantly. But I believe it took me being honest with my thoughts and feelings toward God to take the first step away from being stuck. He did not fall off His throne when I said I really didn't like him anymore. No, He responded with love.

"God, my God, I yelled for help and you put me together. God, you pulled me out of the grave, gave me another chance at life when I was down-and-out......The nights of crying your eyes out give way to days of laughter." Psalms 30:2

# 34

## LIFE CAME FAST— AND WENT FULL CIRCLE

"Life came fast, and with it Pain. When Pain comes knocking, we have two choices: to mask our Pain or to move toward our Pain."[1] Our lives had been moving fast with pain before the husband and I met. It had only sped up after the marriage. There is no denying that the passing of one child puts stress on the marriage. Multiply that by three within a four- year time span. The years of hurricane sized storms we had endured made it difficult when we would try to share our hearts with each other. One could not hear the other through the layers of shock and pain.

We remained wounded with the residue of the deaths our children and that lengthy lawsuit. We stayed busy with the new house, the new dogs and motorcycle rides. It was easy to be social and energetic around our friends. However, when we found ourselves alone, the communication became shallow. We continued to move away from the hurt instead of toward it.

It is often easy to hurt together but nearly impossible to grieve together. It's hard to get close to the deep personal thoughts and feelings that race through another person's mind. Words cannot adequately articulate through the fog of those thoughts. Deep communication was a lost art between the husband and myself. We were both either too stubborn or prideful to get professional help. We had built a life of numbing pain together and the easiest route was to continue that path.

Our personalities were entirely different so we grieved in entirely different ways. I jumped on the corporate ladder and started climbing. I found peace in meeting new people, exploring new places, reaching goals and helping others attain their goals as well. I was offered a corporate position that involved a large percentage of travel. After three years of trying to grieve together that offer was very appealing. I must admit, I saw that opportunity as my *get out of jail free card.*

The husband's response to grief was entirely different. He was continually lost in deep thought. He was very sociable in a crowd but when it came to being alone he went to low places. Over time the low places became more frequent. Before long the depression was unsurmountable. My career was bringing in a sufficient income so his choice was to leave his job and attempt to build a business from home. The odds were against that because that allowed even more time alone to dig deeper into depression. The computer became his closest friend.

So, there we were. Grief and pain had exposed and pushed us into our survival modes. In my mind, I was being the responsible one carrying the financial load and keeping the practical parts of life stable. Climbing the corporate ladder was satisfying my natural drive. Deep thinking and hours of computer time was occupying the husband. He had lost what drive for life he had.

My career soon required a move to Chicago. Even though I loved our house, it had become a maintenance liability. Chicago offered more photography opportunities so I was praying it would give the husband a new vision. However, it proved to be more than the marriage could survive.

I only increased my travel while the husband dug deeper into the computer. I begged him to get a job at a local coffee shop if for no other reason than the socialization. The discussion of counseling for his depression remained a frequent topic. I was open to going together or him going alone. He didn't want to go to a church counselor so I got names of other services. The choice was his. It would only take a little motivation to get the ball rolling. My *cheerleading* with him became a source of anger and he was too deep in depression to take the initiative himself. I would say nothing changed but nothing in a marriage ever stays the same. The only thing left of the marriage was an occasional weekend under the same roof and conversations about bills.

I never saw myself as a divorced person because divorce went against my religious upbringing. The thought of divorce was tormenting because the Bible says God hates divorce. For all the divorced people reading this...Yes God does hate divorce. It breaks his heart to see any of his children hurting. But divorce is not an unforgivable sin. Unfortunately, it has become so common place in our society, people are not nearly as tormented by the thought of it as I was.

So, there we were. I had let my words of healing get snatched away with my career and the frustration with the husband. I had renewed my thoughts of God just waiting to *get me*. In my mind this was God's trick He was playing on me. I had to live in hell on earth or look at divorce. If I chose divorce what punishment from God would I receive for that? Damned if I did and Damned if I didn't.

The promise of healing, I received that stormy night I prayed, grew dim with daily routines. Bitterness was swelling inside me. I resented working and carrying the financial load alone while the husband sat at home on the computer. I kept hearing that voice inside reminding me, "I just need the faith the size of a mustard seed." Oh, I heard it alright but I was totally ignoring it. It is so easy to give up when circumstances don't change immediately. That thought was strong one day and forgotten the next. Even faith as small as a mustard seed requires *giving* it to God to work with. I was comfortable holding on to my little bit of faith and trying to work with it on my own.

I was only required to be in the office in Chicago three days a month for back to back board meetings so I no longer needed to fly home on weekends. I took that opportunity to stay over weekends between trips. I took advantage of being in different regions of this beautiful country and enjoying as many sights as I possibly could. My mom was having some health issues so flying in and out of the Knoxville area became frequent. I began finding

DEBRA HAYES

peace and hope being around my Tennessee family and Lucas on a more regular basis.

Jeff and Tesha had a little rental house in my hometown where I could land between trips. This would give me more access to mom while the doctors tried to locate her problem. More importantly, I was thinking moving out of the apartment in Chicago may jar the husband back into the land of the living. Now seriously...what was I thinking? I was never there anyway. I have no idea why I thought where I was when I wasn't there would make any difference. The only significant factor was that when the lease ran out in Chicago it would not be renewed. That would force the husband to make decisions. His computer addiction had become something I could no longer support.

I talked with him and explained that I was going to be staying in Tennessee from August to December, except the few days I had to be in the office. I would take care of the bills and expenses in both places but he needed to begin thinking about what he wanted to do when the lease ran out.

I was looking forward to having my BMW motorcycle with me in the mountains of Eastern Tennessee and Western North Carolina during the fall months. I left my car in Tennessee and flew to Chicago to get the bike. The husband didn't believe me when I told him I was riding the bike back to Tennessee. He was in denial of several things so me riding five hundred miles in one day on the 1981 R65 easily made it into the brewing pot of denial.

As the time grew nearer for me to pull out of the driveway the reality hit him that I was serious. The bike had two hard bags and a tank bag. I had packed them so full I doubt I could have added a hair pin. I am not sure if he was more concerned for my safety or just wanted to take a long bike ride but regardless, he got his BMW K1 loaded and left on the journey with me. 12 o'clock noon.... Chicago...Five hundred miles...sore butt...tired neck and shoulders...Arrived....2AM...Morristown TN.

The lease ran out in Dec.2004 and the husband moved in with his family also living in Morristown. Our friendship was sparked again as he would come over to visit with the dogs.

I was getting relief from carrying the large financial load. The accompanying freedom was extremely refreshing. We could enjoy each other's company on a shallow level but when the conversation turned toward the storms we lived through, we both froze, put up guards, and went back into survival mode. I could not look back or even think about working though that mountain of pain to make the relationship work. Could that relationship have been restored? Most likely. Did we again run from the pain instead of toward it? Absolutely! I proceeded with the divorce. It was very mutual and simple. By then, we didn't have any children or property and the dogs could not be entered for custody. It was over quickly.

The judge that signed the divorce decree was the same judge that oversaw the bridesmaid's dresses case. He was a friend so after he signed the decree I couldn't help but say, "Well, you saw this thing go full circle." The husband and I rode together to the courthouse that morning then after the divorce was final we went together to spend the afternoon in Gatlinburg. Talk about full circle!!

Yes, that seems weird that we spent an afternoon together the day of our divorce. We are both good people. Life hit us hard. The marriage may not have been a mistake but we both sure make a lot of mistakes trying to survive it.

The husband did eventually reach out for help. He pulled his life together and quickly met a lady who became his wife. She is a beautiful lady with a kind and caring heart. I can say with all the sincerity in my heart that I wish every ounce of happiness on them that a marriage can hold.

# PART THREE
## SITTING

*"So many lies live on this earth,
only through your truth I can discern"*

Collin Raye, "Undefeated"

# 35

## SITTING—
## NECESSARY, YET HAZARDOUS

A couple of definitions of Sitting (per google) are: "A continuous period of being seated and engaged in a particular activity; be or remain in a particular position or state." Sitting should only be used for brief times of rest. It has been documented that some of the health hazards of sitting too long on the natural body are heart disease, overactive pancreas, colon cancer, foggy brain, strained neck, sore shoulders and back, mushy abs, tight hips, limp glutes, poor circulation in legs, soft bones, inflexible spine disk damage and a much higher mortality rate. [1]

There are also spiritual hazards to sitting. I learned that trying to settle in a place that was only meant to be temporary can become very frustrating. Don't get me wrong, life can be full there, but not fulfilled.

I think again of a child in their progress of movement. It is necessary to sit, but they cannot continue to do so all their lives. Sitting is a necessity because it gives them a chance to regroup between their crawling destinations. It gives them a chance to rest and absorb everything around them. Yet, sitting will never take them to the places they need to go. If a person remains in a seated position, they will inevitably become helpless and needy.

There is no better definition for the few years that followed my divorce than SITTING. I had moved back to Tennessee to be near family. The shockwaves had finally ceased from my life in Ohio and Chicago. An uneventful life of settling down was very appealing.

I found myself *sitting* amongst an enormous amount of activity for about six years. Even though I wanted to settle there, God had other plans. Let there be no doubt, when it is time to RISE, God will part the waters of circumstances that seem to be against you. If you follow Him, you will land exactly where you need to be.

# 36

## DAMMED UP EMOTIONS—
## FINALLY ESCAPED

The divorce was final. I had settled back into my hometown thinking that would be my last move. The storms of life had finally calmed but the mask I had been wearing was now dividing my life. When I looked in the mirror I saw a lady who was inferior to all her peers. Most of my friends had successfully executed a normal life with a husband and children. Yet, at that time, all I had to show for myself was a prosperous career.

The United States and Canada had become my office. Mexico, my playground. I was fortunate to be able to prepare my own schedule. Most of our franchises were successful and didn't require a lot of attention. Therefore, my schedule was built around where I desired to go. In the middle of the winter, I could always find a reason to go to our Idaho location. Followed by a weekend of skiing in Sun Valley. On the other hand, if I wanted beach time, San Diego or Fort Myers could be the destination of need.

Mexico was where we took most of our reward trips. Meetings and parties took me there four to five times a year. One of my favorite memories was taking about thirty top producers on an island excursion. We rode catamarans to an island. The day was spent playing in the ocean and relaxing in hammocks. Locals made a large pot of Paella on the beach. The life I lived was an easy one to escape into. Another vivid memory was of a private dinner for corporate employees literally on the beach. Our table was set in the sand facing the water. We were served an exquisite meal and wonderful vintage wine as we watched the sunset.

Each Monday I flew to a designated destination. Once the plane moved to the tarmac for take-off I became an independent goal driven person with a definite purpose. I knew that character well and knew exactly how to perform to my advantage. As the plane hit the tarmac on the return flight, I became lower than a grasshopper in my own eyes. The world offered adventure while my hometown seemed to be a large mirror forcing me to look behind the mask.

One of the nicest things about being home was having *drop in* company. My little white cottage style house was conveniently located on a dead- in street in the middle of town. Buster and Maggie had been away from their two- acre yard long enough to adjust to this small setting. The driveway went down the entire side of the house and ended at a detached garage. On the far edge of the driveway was a basketball goal which offered the perfect place for Buster to be hooked outside. His long cable provided him with outdoor roaming freedoms while keeping my little explorer safe from traffic.

The dogs undoubtedly thought when we had visitors, they had come entirely to play with them. One by one, Buster and Maggie would fetch their toys, lay them at the feet of my guest, looking up as if to say: "Oh you don't like that one? Wait …. I have more." Then they sprinted through the house only to return with another toy. Buster usually got hooked outside for the comfort of my guest. By separating them, Maggie took her docile position at my feet.

One day I as I was walking a friend to their car, we noticed the empty cable laying by the basketball goal. The yard was empty, the carport was empty, and Buster was nowhere to be found. I ran around the yard and into the street in a panic. I yelled his name but no response. Granted, by nature, bulldogs are stubborn so it was not uncommon for him to totally ignore me while he was exploring. I searched through the neighbor's yards and knocked on doors in hope he had charmed his way into their homes. NOTHING… NADA….ZILCH!

My subconscious fear of loss exploded like a raging volcano. Where was Buster? Had someone stolen him? Had he wandered off and been hit by a car?

I called my mom at work crying so frantically she barely understood me. She immediately left to come to my aid. Tesha had also dropped everything she was doing to join the search. She brought Lucas and they drove around scouting the neighborhoods. Mom manned the phone by calling every veterinarian and shelter in the area. While Tesha went southeast, I went northwest. Luke sat in her backseat in his car seat. His little head was just tall enough to peep out the windows. He was approximately three years old and had known Buster and Maggie all his life. Determined to find Buster, he got the Styrofoam cup left from lunch and poked a hole through the bottom. This immediately became his telescope. He held the cup up to his eyes, frantically peering through the window yelling, "Whera ar u Bussa?"

A couple of hours had passed and I returned home down trodden. Finally, a return call came from the shelter telling us their truck had picked up a bulldog. "Sure, He has one white paw and three brindle paws. He has a white face and two brindle ears. When you say bye-bye, those ears will stand erect," I said fighting through the tears. I could see the smile on the lady's face through the relieved tone in her voice. "Yes, I believe we have your dog."

They had picked him up at the bank located between my house and moms'. Her house was less than a mile from mine and the dogs loved staying there.

Evidently, when I hooked Buster up that afternoon, I did not get the cable latched. He had decided to visit mom. He made his way through my neighborhood, through a large grocery store parking lot, across a busy four lane highway, and was meandering through the bank parking lot when he was *arrested for trespassing*.

By now, I had gathered my composure but Tesha insisted on driving to pick up Buster. (That girl always has my back.) Mom kept Lucas while we went to get Buster out of jail. The truck arrived at least 30 minutes before we did. The echoing sound of dogs barking met us as we opened the door to the small office. I listened closely to recognize the bark that was all too familiar. Suddenly, right in front of me, two paws hit the top of a desk and a little brindle head popped up with excitement. Those big brown eyes looked at me as if to say: "HEY MOM, I took a ride in a truck." Within minutes of the truck's arrival he had stolen the hearts of the office girls. One lady told me if I hadn't made it in, he was going home with her.

One would think that after the losses I had been through with my boys, misplacing Buster for the afternoon would pale in comparison. Unfortunately, raw wounds do not make comparisons. Anything large or small can trigger unresolved pain.

Later that day I gathered Buster and Maggie and went to moms' house to spend the night. The tears that had been triggered that afternoon began to swell like a tsunami. *Uncontrollable* could not even begin to describe the flood of grief that had just been released. This went on for hours. I would wear myself down then begin the whole tsunami of tears again. "When was the last time you had a good cry?" mom asked. Well, I didn't remember having had a full-blown cry. Sure, I had wept over the years but never treated myself to a long, uninterrupted, deep felt, satisfying cry. With the babies, I was mostly in shock and depression. With Randall, I felt I had to be the strong one so I never slowed down and gave time to rushing tears. With Stefan, that mask was so tightly embedded that a tear could not trickle down my face. The afternoon episode with Buster had breached the dam.

This continued for days. I was scheduled to do a long motorcycle trip that weekend but cancelled to stay home and cry. Years of dammed up emotions took about five days to escape.

Crying is a natural course for healing. Do not ever be ashamed or feel weak because you cry. It is more damaging to hold it inside. Just as water cleanses the outside of our bodies, our tears have the same inside effect on our souls.

Tears are words the heart can't express. ~ Author Unknown

What soap is for the body, tears are for the soul. ~ Jewish Proverb

# 37

## I TRADED A WEEKEND
## WITH KEVIN COSTNER—
## FOR THIS?

Life on the road, even with all its perks, was beginning to wear on me. I was connecting with my roots in Tennessee and it was becoming harder to leave. When my work was within five to six hours, I chose to drive instead of fly. Buster usually made the trip with me. He was an excellent traveler and a welcomed guest by most of the franchisees. Maggie wasn't as fond of the car. Her position for riding was always in the front floor board with her nose pressed forward toward the air vent. Her rump and back legs had their perfect fit against the passenger seat. Buster would occupy that seat in an upright position as not to miss anything going by the window. Therefore, Maggie rarely made the business trips.

My company frequently sponsored events. Some more interesting than others. A celebrity golf tournament in South Carolina, where I was slotted to be the corporate rep, was ranking high on the calendar. It was basically in the backyard of one of my favorite franchisees so this event had been surrounded with lots of anticipation and preparation.

Our equipment team from Chicago had trucked materials earlier in the week. There was no need for me to arrive until Thursday evening. I needed to arrive just in time for the private cocktail party with the celebrities and other sponsors. That gave me plenty time to pick the perfect outfits and swirl around in the whirlwinds of indecision of what to wear. Each day for an entire week I changed my mind, so six new outfits became crucial purchases.

I had worked with numerous motivational speakers, entertainers, and TV personalities at our corporate conferences over the years. I didn't know why this one was tripping me. Yes, I did! Kevin Costner was going to be there and I was a huge fan!!!! For years, *Tin Cup*[1] had been one of my go to movies just to laugh. The weekend was going to begin with a small private cocktail party of forty people or less. In attendance would be, not only Jamie Farr, but......yes... Kevin Costner.

I had gotten a few painful cramps in my side over the weekend as I rode my motorcycle. That was weird. I was relatively healthy and, other than the birth of the babies, no health issue had ever slowed me down. Maybe I had been on the bike in one position too long? Yep, that was probably it.

On Monday afternoon, I doubled over again with my side. This time I diagnosed myself as having eaten something that disagreed with me. The pain came and went but when it hit, it hit hard. Still convinced it would pass, I kept the countdown ticking toward Thursday night. Every accessorized detail had been packed for days.

Thursday morning started with a few hard pains. The drive to South Carolina was only a couple of hours and I was leaving early enough to make sure our Chicago team had everything in place. The pains hit so hard it brought tears to my eyes as I drove south on I-81 and merged onto I-40 East. I pulled to the side of the highway. The county hospital was only a few minutes away so I'd quickly stop by the ER, get some treatment, and be on my way. It had to be something simple that could be easily treated. Right?

As usual, when sitting in any waiting room, the race with the clock was on. Fortunately, (or so I thought at the time) a severe pain hit and I was taken directly into a room. I bypassed even the triage stop. Several test results were threatening overnight observation. WHAT? The only observation I wanted that night was with Kevin Costner.... up close and personal.

I tried to explain my urgency. If they would just prescribe something to get me through the weekend, I'd spend an entire week with them when I returned. I would also agree to be tested and poked to their satisfaction. The afternoon was ticking away, the hospital staff was moving in slow motion, and the writing on the wall was becoming clear.

I could not believe I was doing it, but I called the Chicago office and explained my situation. I suggested they fly someone to the tournament, just in case I could not escape from my jail of infirmity. It would be better to have two reps on location than none. Knowing me as well as they did, they knew it had to be a dire situation for me to be making THAT call.

ARE YOU KIDDING ME????? It MAY be my gall bladder? So, what about, it may NOT be my gall bladder? Couldn't they give me something for the pain until next week? My enzymes were up and so was my time. I tried to convince them that I drank wine the night before. (That happened to be a lie at the time). They surely must know the enzymes would go back down by drinking lots of water.

The pain became more severe with each lie I told in the case I was trying to build. Pinocchio's nose had nothing on my lies and the increasing pain in my side. The more lies I told to lessen the appearance of my condition, the worse the pain became. The surgeon had been called, the operating room reserved, and my gall bladder was on its' way out. Kevin Costner would be sporting cocktails and golf clubs for the weekend while I would be sporting hospital food and an opened back gown. Not quite the sexy outfit I had prepared.

I was certainly no stranger to worse hospital situations than this, but heck...What a disappointment!

# 38

## THAT LESSON—
## WAS STILL AHEAD

I would pay the ex-husband to care for the dogs while I was traveling. Buster had seemed to be losing quite a bit of weight so he was taken in to be checked. After the examination, the ex was told that Buster was simply missing his mama. He was attached to me, so we bought it. He had also begun showing signs of needing help getting into the bed. (Buster, not the ex) Normally, he was like a gazelle. Lately, however, he had begun waiting at the side of the bed for help to get in. Both dogs slept with me and it was quite strange that Maggie was presuming dominance on the mattress while Buster stood in the floor. I assumed he was acting needy for the extra attention.

Another time I had left them with Mom. She had Buster outside on a leash doing his business in the rain. She was more anxious to go back inside than he was. As she leaned down to get his collar and turn him toward the house, he snapped at her. That was totally out of character. He loved her and had never snapped at anyone. When I got home from that trip I noticed his ribs showing. Holy Cow!!! I had been traveling for years. My absence was not causing this.

A trip to the animal hospital revealed that the veterinarian who originally saw him was newly out of school. He had not even performed blood work. Upon further examination, I was told that Busters' stomach was full of cancerous tumors. They were too numerous to remove. This explained his unusual behaviors. I watched him get weaker over the next couple of weeks. The decision was obvious upon the return visit to the animal hospital. The ex-husband met me there. We looked at each other with tears in our eyes as we held Buster. Once more, we were saying goodbye to a piece of our heart. Even though this was a pet and not a child, when your heart is attached, it hurts.

I must say the ex was much braver than I that day. Buster had filled a void in my empty heart and a place in my empty arms but I was not strong enough to stay in the room with him. My ex, did not leave his side until his suffering came to an end.

Life keeps coming even when you just want to scream... ENOUGH!

I soon left my position in Chicago to do independent consulting. I took a contract in Greenville, South Carolina. I would live there while I helped the franchisees develop their business and train their staff. It was only two to three hours from my hometown. The owners were close friends. It was a beautiful city and the contract was only for six months. There were also friends in the area I had known since high school. The move was a very comfortable one. I rented a small apartment and Maggie and I landed in South Carolina.

I didn't realize this move would expose the mask of self-condemnation I hid behind. I had been trying to fill my hole of low self-esteem with other people. Leaving the familiarity of my hometown caused me to begin the search for what exactly it was going to take to rid myself of the guilt I carried. For the first time since tragedy after tragedy stormed my life, I wasn't in survival mode. I was by myself and beginning to ponder my future.

I would frequently let my thoughts drift back to the night I knew I heard God tell me He could heal me with faith the size of a mustard seed. The truth behind that was something I had not yet learned. Sure, I didn't have any trouble believing He could. Would He? I wasn't sure. I wasn't seeing any evidence of it so far. My heart had moved past the dark place of ending it all but it certainly wasn't at peace. I was still searching.

I continued to believe that my punishment for Stefan had manifested when I said good bye to Ephraim, Isaac and Randall. I was praying that punishment had come to an end. Could that be what He meant by healing me? Maybe He only meant that I would not get punished anymore and I could begin to live a life of status quo. Quite frankly, at that moment, status quo was far above the life I had lived the previous decade. I knew He was there and I was trying hard to convince myself that He was a good God. My communication with God was me basically doing all the talking. I was trying desperately to rebuild my life, myself.

There are two ways to begin the day in prayer. *1. I've Got This. But, I Could Use Some Help.* When approaching prayer this way it is more like having a board meeting with God. You fill Him in on the details of the day and give Him his duties. (Lord, I'm doing this, this and this and I need your help here and here). I'm not in any way saying He doesn't hear this prayer and I'm not in any way saying He won't get involved and answer your request. I am saying that it puts Him in a box. *2. Humbly Expressing Need.* This is the prayer a humble man prays realizing his complete dependency upon God. (Lord, I have no idea what this day will hold but I invite you into it to lead me and show me the way.)

I admit at that point in my life my prayers were more like a board meeting than sincerely seeking. The lesson I needed to learn was to quit trying to get Him to bless what I was doing and simply get on board with what He was doing. Because....it was already blessed!

That was a lesson that was still ahead of me.

# 39

## MY RELATIONSHIP WITH GOD—
## WAS BIPOLAR

M y relationship with God was bipolar. Not from His perspective but from mine. I was trying hard. In fact, my efforts to find peace were exhausting. Thoughts would fluctuate from extreme optimism to deep doubts. Hopeful that life was heading in a new direction yet trapped in my own limiting beliefs. Prayer, or should I say, *spiritual begging*, became a routine as I took my daily walks. Walking for miles and talking to God gave me time to pour out my thoughts. In addition, I would quote scripture, quote more scripture, even fast at times, while waiting for God to change my circumstances. When my prayers were not answered as I wanted, my frustration would dig up familiar doubts. Those doubts would always ask the questions, "Could God really have a future FOR ME?"

My mask was still in place but beginning to shift. Confidence radiated on the outside while uncertainty jabbed on the inside. The years I had spent in my business gave me boldness with anything pertaining to work. I would walk into the office with confidence but doubts would weaken me when I was alone. After settling into a routine in South Carolina with my new friends, it didn't take long to identify my distractions and the root of my poor self-image. People who knew absolutely nothing about the storms in my life were quick to point out a toxic relationship I had let myself get caught in *again*.

I had become reacquainted with Stefan's father upon returning to my hometown after the divorce. Initially, we had conversations about that horrible decision we made years before. We were both remorseful and asked forgiveness. The words were no doubt sincere but not enough to unmask the shame, guilt, and self-condemnation I lived with.

When looking through a mask, oftentimes, the eye holes are too small to see the full picture of the surrounding reality. I began spending time with that man when I first moved back to my hometown. Common interest kept us busy. An occasional trip down memory lane was somewhat comforting in a weird sort of way. Looking backwards is beneficial if you want to gain perspective. However, it is never a good idea to try to recreate those times and camp there.

I spent the next six years of my life being distracted from receiving the healing I was searching for. God had told me he would heal me but I proceeded to conclude the way he was going to do it. In my opinion, the healing and forgiveness would be complete if the relationship with the baby's father would work out. Go to the root of the problem and heal from there. Right? Learning the lesson of getting on board with God's direction, instead of doing my own daily *spiritual begging* about that relationship, cost me years. I probably missed healthy relationships I could have had along the way. I did eventually walk away from that situation (story to follow) thanking God for saying *NO*.

It is only natural whenever we hear the word *No* to think it is a negative thing. The first reaction to the word *No* is usually a mental shield. It almost always means we are not going to get our way about something. I learned that a *No* from God only meant that He knew me better than I knew myself, and that He wanted more for me than I would allow myself to dream. My own limiting beliefs kept me in a whirlwind of distraction.

In the meantime, I completed the contract in South Carolina and moved back to Tennessee. After sixteen years in the same career, I began looking for a different challenge instead of a different contract. I had a dear friend that had recently moved back from Georgia. Sharing stories of her life in Atlanta and mine in Chicago left us with the common frustration of small town living versus the big city energy.

She had a concept for a show called "Two Chicks About Town." Videos were becoming the rage so we jumped on board. That decision was made from boredom early one Friday afternoon. By 6PM that evening we had bought a camera, a tripod, microphones, and parked ourselves outside the gate at the local football stadium. East High School and West High School were playing the annual town rival game that night. What better place to begin our new adventure? We had a blast *interviewing* the crowd as they entered the stadium. We had gone to school with many of the patrons so it was effortless to grab someone to talk to. Our little video segments aired locally on an internet channel and began gaining followers.

At the same time, the local electric company, who owned the local cable channel, was signing a contract with an out of town gentleman to do local advertisement. Another development on the table was to build a hometown TV Channel. A "Two Chicks" follower sent videos of our little *escape from boredom* show which resulted in an interview/meeting. The initial interest was for me to host some of the segments for the new local channel. After learning of my extensive experience, I was hired not only to host but to do the sales and marketing to build the concept for the channel.

The money was nowhere near what I was used to making. But the challenge was something I could not say no to.

# 40

## DEAD END DISTRACTIONS—
## TIME TO ELIMINATE

The hometown channel had just the right boundaries to make it successful. It was upbeat and positive. The best part was, there was to be no news, weather, religion, politics, or platforms for town issues. The citizens of the town were to be the stars of the show. That was accomplished with a continuous twenty- hour loop that included several three to five minute segments. It was all supported by local advertisement.

What a FUN job! Yes, it certainly offered the challenge I was looking for. No doubt, I traded financial security for fun. The channel immediately took a humorous, you never know what to expect, flavor when a high school friend did the very first "Behind the Scenes" with me. (A "Behind the Scenes" was about a five- minute segment. We would visit the business and find creative ways to highlight it to the community.) He owned a pharmacy and, by the end of his segment, we were talking and laughing about a suppository called a Rectal Rocket. (https://youtu.be/3TbwsM-1gGw).

The relationships I built and the people I became acquainted with were precious to me. They were the greatest asset of the job. It was an honor to give the townspeople an opportunity to "be on TV". Some of the best segments were with children. One of my favorites was when we accompanied and filmed a trip to an *Atlanta Braves* baseball game with the Boys and Girls Club. For most of these children, it was the first time they had been to a big city or a major sporting event. (https://youtu.be/1ezKK_nW9Ck)

Anytime you put yourself in the public eye, be ready for criticism. The show had only been on the air about a month or so when one morning I woke up with a migraine. Ball cap, hair in pony tail, tee shirt, yoga pants, no make-up, and glasses instead of contacts was a typical look for someone going to the store for meds.... don't you think? An older couple behind me obviously was having problems with their hearing aids because their whispers carried across two aisles. "There is that girl on Channel 7. She sure looks better on TV than she does in person." Seriously? A stranger recognized me? My first reaction was to say something like, "You'd look this bad too if you felt the way I do today." My second thought was maybe I shouldn't have left the house without *gusseying up* a bit. (a southern term for dressing up). But then I just chuckled, shook my head, and thought, "Well.... at least I know people are watching."

That four- year venture on television brought lots of laughter, touching moments, new friendships, and valuable education about the area where I was raised. In one episode, I was fortunate to interview several of my Daddy's football buddies. Our culture center was adding a Sports Hall of Fame and Daddy was being inducted. WOW!! I would never have guessed, when I took that position, I would be spending an afternoon with Daddy's football buddies. I heard story after story of his high school days. *The more I learned about my father, the more it defined who I was.* For years to come, I would find that also to be true with my Heavenly Father.

Being on TV took the mask that was beginning to shift and placed it securely back over my eyes. Sometimes I would watch the channel and think to myself, "I like that girl I see on TV, I wish I were her all the time." I was happy, secure, and having fun when I was in the public eye. But when I had time alone, I picked that load of self-condemnation right back up and toted it around. Would I ever be able to get out from under that guilt I carried?

My performance orientation was peaking and the inner struggle was growing. On the one hand, I was doing a job that came natural to me and loving every minute of it. On the other hand, I was still drowning in the distraction of spending time with Stefan's father. Close friends and family were constantly giving me advice and trying to open my eyes to just how toxic that relationship was. Somehow, I still held tight to the twisted deception that if that relationship would only work, God's forgiveness would somehow be complete. Granted, we had fun together but it was going nowhere. It had become a Dead- End Distraction.

Ever feel like your life goes in endless circles?

Sometimes the circles are filled with fun and energy. Other times, the circles are filled with pain and disappointments. Either way, we seem to end up back in the same place with no progress.

Let's take a quick look at it.

A Dead End is something that has no exit. It is a position that offers no hope of progress. A good example would be a Cul-De-Sac.

Distraction is an interruption, an obstacle to concentration.

Do you have a Dead- End Distraction that keeps you from making progress in your life? Could it be a person or relationship that continually drains all your energy? Could it be a job that is so comfortable the familiarity won't conquer the fear of going for your dream? Could it be a group of people that give you a continuous flow of laughter and warm acceptance yet offer no hope for that deep longing inside?

The first step to progress is to identify your Dead- End Distractions. To have new scenery you must get off that cul-de-sac of familiarity. You should take some risks traveling down new roads. Sometimes, that distraction is something you need to eliminate completely. If that person or situation is toxic to your life, eliminate!!!

When you prioritize your life, you will quickly recognize the difference between a Dead- End Distraction and a healthy diversion. A healthy diversion isn't toxic. It is simply the place you go to destress.

Keep in mind, a dead end doesn't always feel like you have hit a brick wall. It won't always look like you are at the end of a road. It is more likely to be fueled with energy. Yet, over time when you measure your progress, you are in the same place, with the same people, doing the same thing, and asking the same questions. Those questions will most likely be rooted in the toxic lies: *I am not enough or I do not have enough.*

I'm certain my toxic lies took root at the time of the abortion. I have no doubt the baby's father reacted out of fear and unresolved pain in his own life. Yet, his quick abandonment of the situation left me thinking, "Why am I not enough to be the mother of his child?" I certainly was enough for the sex. "Why have I never been enough to be a priority with him?" My only priority took place under the sheets. The twisted deception was that I would find my answers with him. Going to the root of a problem brings resolve but when you misidentify the root, it only delays the answers. I soon learned that the root problem did not lie in the relationship with this man but in my own understanding of forgiveness.

I finally recognized my own Dead- End Distraction the night he said to me, "If anyone ever treated my daughter the way I treat you, I'd kill him." Seriously?? He admitted the toxicity in the relationship but was perfectly comfortable with it? WAKE UP CALL!!!! I was beginning to see what friends had been telling me. It was indeed time to eliminate!

Along with the realization that I needed to eliminate the relationship, I had to also own the fact that it did not get to that point overnight. *We teach people how to treat us.* That is the profound truth. I had allowed myself to remain with someone who I knew treated me like an option and not a priority. I knew I was only holding a spot on his social calendar while he continued to look for someone better. Sure, his comparing remark of someone treating his daughter the same way was hurtful and sounded cruel. The reality was, years of me not standing up for myself and hoping things would change had ushered it in.

The rut of familiarity is often a hard one to climb out of. Once truth hits our brain, we do not automatically have the strength and courage to make changes. Nothing changes when we sit and hope. We must begin to move. Right doors will begin to open if we are willing to take the first steps.

I was, no doubt, stuck but was beginning to look at changing the outlook toward my future. I wanted to eliminate that relationship but the familiarity kept me bound. I never regretted the friendship but I certainly regretted the decisions made and the time I wasted in it. It is difficult to cut something or someone out of your life when there isn't anything or anyone to fill the void. The truth is "once people begin unmasking their painkillers, they gain new courage."[1]

# 41

## THE CALM—
## BEFORE ANOTHER STORM

The TV channel was growing along with my responsibilities. It was occupying most of my time and was an excellent outlet to refocus my energy. Facebook was also growing exponentially. The excitement of reconnecting with school friends and chatting with co-workers from my travels filled the time that I wasn't working. One evening I reconnected with a junior high sweetheart.

It wasn't long before our Facebook chats turned into two or three- hour phone conversations. Nor was it long before I realized that I liked the way I was being treated. He made me feel special and seemed to appreciate me for just being me. Maybe that was another divine appointment of exactly who I needed, exactly when I needed him. That relationship began at age twelve. There was something invigorating about reflecting backwards to a point in my life that was so innocent.

Our new videographer with the channel became one of my best friends. Chris was the real deal. He was a strong Christian man who never presented himself anything but. He was married and became another brother figure in my life. His sense of humor mirrored mine so creating content was effortless. Working together became a continuous flow of laughter. There is more power than most people realize in the truth that laughter is the best medicine.

The channel grew so fast I found myself spending most my time with administrative duties. None of which were the sources of my income. My personal wages came solely from the ad sales. I had built the accounts to a level of maintenance. Which meant by the time I properly served those clients, helped design concepts, filmed, proofed edits, scheduled and ran production days, I did not have time to prospect new accounts. Yet, I was doing what I loved and I was putting 110% into it. The income was barely enough to cover bills and the savings account was dwindling fast. I had spent over a decade in Corporate America, yet, I did not use any of that negotiating knowledge when I took the position. I was too excited to be finally establishing myself (or so I thought) back in my hometown. Fascination with tackling a new and exciting challenge tossed common sense right out the window.

My contract was not with the electric company, as most people thought. It was with the gentleman the electric company had contracted. This was a business he had done successfully for years, however, he did it for someone else. He was now venturing out on his own. His vision was easy to connect with. We all talked big dreams. Working together was lively and entertaining but we did not have capital behind us. It was a make it or break it venture and we had made it......so far. Chris and I would constantly laugh saying, "Imagine what we could do if we had capital, a crew, sales people, a little clerical help, an office or even a green screen." We worked entirely from his van and laptops but we had successfully connected with our audience and turned the channel into the buzz of the town.

Even though the electric company had eyes on everything we did, it was our responsibility to monitor the channel. Chris lived an hour away and the gentleman we contracted with lived five hours away. The channel was not accessible from my house in the county and certainly not accessible from their locations. I would spend hours upon hours in the lobby at a local hotel watching and monitoring the channel.

As I mentioned earlier, one of the nicest benefits of the position was meeting new people. Many of our viewers sought us out, as was the case with an extremely nice real estate broker. As I got to know him better, he offered to let me use his house to monitor instead of frequently hanging out in the hotel lobby. That friendship grew but we both had crazy schedules. It was a task finding quality time together. He gave me his gate code and garage code so I could pop in whenever I needed to monitor.

My days were filled with laughing with Chris, chatting on the phone with my junior high school sweetheart, and spending time with my new real estate buddy. I was enjoying the honest and sincere value I was receiving from these three guys. I had less and less time for Stefan's dad. It was becoming an easy parting of the ways.

All the pleasantries I was experiencing was only the calm before another storm.

I needed to find a way to take the channel to the next level for more income. The house I owned as well as my two motorcycles, my Mercedes and my RX 7 convertible had become a maintenance liability so I began to sell things off. The convertible was the first to go. I had become so emotionally involved with the channel that I was not thinking with good business sense. It was like birthing a child. Watching it grow from infancy left no room for entertaining the thought of walking away. I felt justified with the sacrifices I was making. Success and failure were sparring in the palm of my hand.

# 42

## WHIRLWINDS—
## FROM EVERY DIRECTION

My finances worsened with the success of the channel. I continued to sell possessions to make ends meet while hanging on to hopes of promotion. The next to go was my red BMW R65 motorcycle. That was a bittersweet day! That was the bike I had learned to ride on and had been my therapy after the babies. Yet, it had become unsafe to ride long distances. The age of the bike was due cause for many things beginning to wear out. I feared getting hundreds of miles away in the Western North Carolina Blue Ridge Mountains and something breaking and leaving me stranded. I rode the BMW around town but would take my Suzuki Katana for long distance rides. That first bike was the one I thought I would always hold onto for sentimental reasons.

I had a large account that went out of business during the middle of winter when ad sales were at their worst and bills were at their peak. I began more than ever playing the *catch up later* game with my bills. Stress and worry over money began to occupy my mind. I had begun letting my phone calls go to voicemail. I never knew if the person on the other side of that number was a new client asking for information or a collector looking for a payment.

One nice diversion was my newly reacquainted junior high sweetheart. He lived in Kentucky in a place I had become familiar with as I would travel between Ohio and Tennessee. The long hours of phone conversations had led to visits. I remember one weekend I went to Kentucky to visit and literally slept about 80% of the time. He was so comfortable to be with. I was away from my stress and BAM I was asleep almost the entire weekend. What graciousness! His only reaction was, "I'm sure you needed to relax and sleep." Yep, there certainly was something cozy and refreshing about being with someone I had known since the age of twelve.

The TV channel was a dead end for me and I was beginning to realize it. I finally took off my blinders and knew something had to change. And change it did. One envelope in the mailbox sent my world into another whirlwind. I had played catch up a few times with my mortgage but had never gotten the foreclosure letter. Fear caused me to shake after I opened the threatening letter. I was shivering to the point that I fully expected armored guards to show up the next day, padlock my house, and leave me sitting in the front yard in a straight back uncomfortable wooden chair with a small suitcase of clothes and my dog at my feet.

By happenstance, about the time I finished reading the letter my real estate friend called. I was in tears and asked if I could come to his house. I took the letter. As he was reading it, he asked me how much my house was worth then asked how much I owed on it. It was worth a significant amount more than I owed. In a firm matter of fact, yet kind, voice he said, *"You might as well start packing your bags. I don't know what kind of hell they will put you through before they take it. But since you are not upside down, they won't turn loose now that you are on the hook. I am seeing this happen all over the country."* Not the insight I hoped for. The letter gave me a few days to respond.

I owed approximately $3000. Some of my TV contracts had renewed and I had $2000 to put toward it. Ignorantly, yet excitedly, I made the phone call to clear the debt. I felt confident that I would get back on track because there was hint in the letter of *working* with me.

"Are you kidding me? You WON'T take my money?" I exclaimed in disbelief as the lady on the other end of the phone explained that I needed to keep my money. They wanted to put me into a loan modification program. Seriously?? I tried to negotiate for twenty- four additional hours, before they started the modification process. I guaranteed them I knew a hundred people that would give me $10. That would be the $1000 I needed to complete the payment. That would not have been my first choice in a course of action, but I was willing to do it. That discussion was quickly shut down. THE GAME WAS ON!!!

My time with Stefan's father had become less frequent but he was not completely out of the picture. There had never been any commitment on his part so I felt no obligation to let him know I was spending time with other guys. Maybe that was my mistake. If he had known, maybe he would not have felt the need to inform me he was getting involved with someone else. The drama that followed became another active whirlwind from a different direction.

The deception of that relationship ever working out had long left my mind. I wasn't exactly sure where my life was headed but I *was* exactly sure where it *wasn't*. A whirlwind of relational drama was the last thing I needed. The financial struggles, the foreclosure war, wondering if I was going to be homeless, and trying to decide on a new source of income was more than enough on my mind. Maybe if I had blatantly announced," *I'm done and I'm moving on*", when I recognized the need to eliminate that relationship, the ridiculous drama that followed could have been avoided. The attention I had previously given him was perceived by some to be a threat to his growing relationship. I felt like I was back in high school with some of the cyber bullying that followed. Some of my IT connections confirmed it was not him sending the emails because the AP addresses were coming from out of town. I didn't want or need to get caught in that web. After a few phone calls, angry words, and tears of frustration both our lives were headed away from each other and in the direction, they should have been going all along.

(I will interject here, if anyone reading this is getting bullied in any way, please speak up and be heard. You are not alone and there is help. Remember the one doing the bullying is the one with the problem. Sometimes people are mean and life sucks but you do not deserve to be bullied. Please reach out for help.)

# 43

## SOMETIMES SALVATION—
## IS IN THE EYE OF THE STORM

*Sometimes Salvation*[1] by the Black Crowes paints a darker picture than what I was dealing with in my life but the message is still the same. Circumstances can begin crumbling all around you but YOU must be the one to take courage and make the changes.

The financial struggle and the foreclosure war continued. I had decided to start teaching exercise classes for extra money. I scheduled a trip to Ohio for certification but at the last minute that class was cancelled. Lexington offered the next closest class a couple of months later so I registered.

In the meantime, while talking with my Kentucky friend, I became curious about the churches that were near the area where he lived. I vividly remember sitting in the den floor one Sunday afternoon with my laptop watching a basketball game. I went online to search churches in Georgetown Kentucky. One stood out so I pulled up the sermons from www.victorylifeonline.com and began listening.

WOW…could this guy be for real? He was extremely direct and his messages clear. Everything he was teaching made me want to jump up and say "YES, finally somebody is offering direct truth that can be applied to crappy life situations." He was not suggesting some *pie in the sky blink your eye and Jesus will fix it* message. But I knew by listening, this guy had lived through some hell himself and was not just handing out religious words. He spoke with deep confidence and conviction. No matter what you are going through there is hope for a better life.

For weeks, I continued to listen to series after series. Disappointments in "God's Persons" in my past had left me skeptical so I searched through the website looking for anything to prove my skepticism. The pastor was nice looking and his wife was beautiful. In my opinion, maybe they were a little too perfect. I bet that was it, He had a strong message but they probably weren't very approachable.

The weekend came to go to Lexington for the exercise certification. After spending two grueling days working out with a room full of girls between the ages of eighteen and twenty, I drove my aching body up the road to locate that Georgetown church I had been listening to. That was late Saturday afternoon. I wanted to scout it out before I committed to visiting the next day.

The church was an old remodeled Kroger building with a very attractive and inviting front. As I was pulling into the parking lot to get a closer look there was a van driving out in the opposite direction. A friendly lady looked over at me, smiled, waved, and drove on. That was a welcome site. (I would give anything now to know who that was.) The exercise experience had not been all I had hoped for. Even though I could hang physically, I felt very misplaced for two days. That smile and wave from the lady in the van was what I needed to convince me to stay the night and visit the church the following morning.

I purposely had not let my friend know I was in town because I was on a mission. I knew I would be exhausted from exercise and I wanted to check out that church without any outside influence. I fully intended to go in, sit in the back, listen to the sermon, and make my judgements. I would then quickly make my way to the parking lot and drive back to Tennessee.

I was right on time driving from Lexington to arrive about 5 minutes before it started and find my back- row seat. Apparently, the traffic was thicker on Saturday evening than Sunday morning so I arrived about 20 minutes before I had planned. As I walked in, I was warmly greeted and introduced to a lady to show me around. I was pleasantly surprised that she only showed me where the bathrooms were and took me to the café to get something to drink.

I was very relaxed with the nonthreatening conversations. She took me over and pointed out the pastor's wife. Yep, she looked exactly like she did online. I fully expected to get the plastic greeting and welcome. As she walked closer I noticed she had on blue jeans and University of Kentucky accessories. Her warm welcome was anything but a plastic performance. She introduced herself as Tracy and engaged in friendly conversation. We connected immediately. She asked if I was alone. As soon as I answered "yes" she insisted I come sit with her.

It was time to begin. "No, bring your drink in with you, we don't care", she said as we moved toward the auditorium. The lights were going down and the music began much like a concert. I followed her as she walked directly to the front row, hugged a few necks, and pointed to our seats. Oh, good grief, instead of slipping into the back row, I was seated in the front row with the pastors' wife.

I was not disappointed at all. In fact, the word REAL was the only way I could describe it. Afterwards, Tracy introduced me to her husband. Gary was also dressed in jeans and was as genuine and sincere in person as he was through his sermons.

We chatted about how I had found them online but I never disclosed the mess I was dealing with in Tennessee. As I was leaving, Tracy made me promise if I was ever in the area again to please come back.

Upon my return to Tennessee, I continued to listen to the sermons online. The skepticism that shielded my ears had been removed and I was hearing Truth that was speaking directly into my struggles. I was not hearing rules or a *Christian Not-To-Do* list. I was hearing God's love and acceptance. Over and over I would be reminded, "There is absolutely no condemnation for those who are in Christ. God is not mad at you. He is not upset with you. He wants nothing but the best for you. He hung on the cross for you and offers forgiveness for everything. He has good plans for you. He will gently lead and guide you through those plans if you seek him."

# 44

## THE BLESSING TRAIN
## IS ON THE WAY—
## CHOO CHOO!!!!

The foreclosure war continued. The promised modification process extended for several months. All the while, they were not taking my money and I was getting further behind. The bank finally came back with concern over my inconsistent income. Where I had been so close to being caught up, I was then being forced to sell my house within the next six months. I quickly got a realtor and put it on the market. With each month that passed, I would get a letter saying the house was to be auctioned off by a third party. The confusing part was each month immediately following **that** letter was another letter. It was from the bank stating they were stopping the auction each month while the house was on the market. How confusing was that? But that was the routine to be followed every single month. It would continue for the duration of the six months I had been given to sell.

Those letters began almost immediately after I had made my visit to the church in Georgetown. It seemed the only clarity in my life came as I listened to the online sermons. I began driving to Kentucky about every three weeks or so to go to church. The drive was a good break from my pressing issues and I began connecting with the Georgetown people. It was almost as if some people had become celebrities. Gary would mention folks in his online sermons. Sitting in the room, I could put faces to those names. "Oh, that is Jack and Rose." "That must be the Ricketts, they have a lot of children and are always at ball parks".

More importantly a friendship with Tracy was developing. One Sunday afternoon we went to lunch and I filled her in on some of the mess I was dealing with in Tennessee. I hated to do that because I didn't want to be perceived as the person who was always talking about their problems. I didn't go into a lot of detail because I was still wearing my mask, even though I could feel God beginning to gently pull it away. She asked for my email to stay in touch. The thought of me moving to Kentucky wasn't even a possibility. That would involve moving cost and finding a job. I was so beaten down that entertaining those thoughts felt like a train wreck.

Tracy and I continued to email. She was sincerely reaching out with words of encouragement for me to hang in there. These are two of the emails we shared:

Me: "I hate to bother you. Please pray. I have never in my life sounded like such a whiner. Just when you think life is heavy, more weight comes. It is SO HARD right now. LOSS seems to be all around me. My heart has become completely disconnected to this town and I feel NO purpose to be here. I am so afraid. Every time I listen to one of Gary's sermons I just want to jump up and say YES. I am so confused right now. I have never been at rock bottom in every area of my life at the same time. I don't even know where I will be in a couple of weeks. I have had my dog for 10 years and I cannot bear the thought of losing her too right now. The apartment mom is getting has two bedrooms but I can't take Maggie there. I am so tired and scared.

Please pray for God to be clear. More so that I would have the ears to hear his direction."

Tracy's response: "My goodness!!! Bless your heart, you sure are facing a lot of difficult situations right now. But sister I KNOW that God is gonna bring you out!!!! You keep your head up, even when it seems like you only have one nostril above the mess, and you feel like you're sinking. You ARE coming out of this, you tell the enemy and everyone else to just watch and see how your God is gonna deliver you!!!! I will be praying for you tonight, and

I am standing with you that God is opening doors right now for you! I know we have only met, but we do have a kindred spirit! And we do know how to stand on the WORD no matter what!!!! You have a good nights' sleep and expect something good to come your way tomorrow. The blessing train is on the way "choo choo." LOL"

It seemed odd to be receiving encouragement from a total stranger who had absolutely nothing to gain. Her simple kindness proved to be the very thing that changed my life forever. It emphasized the difference between relationship and religion. She didn't care that I wasn't a church member. She didn't care that I lived two hundred miles away. She didn't care that no one was aware of her outreach to me. She simply loved the Lord and wanted to share His love. Her interest was in my relationship with Him not in my involvement at Victory Life Church.

You see, I had been going to a church in Tennessee for about three years. One evening I ran into that Pastor on a hospital visit with a friend. After he asked me how I was doing, I told him I was in the middle of losing everything. His answer was, "Yeah I heard about that". Quite honestly, I was a little hurt with that answer. He didn't even bother to offer me a prayer. Though I was a little hurt, I wasn't angry. I had learned through my previous dealings with some Pastors that my trust was in God, not in man.

On one hand, I had a Pastor and his wife two hundred miles away, who didn't know me, emailing me and encouraging me. They were building my faith that God would make a way when there seemed to be no way. They were giving me Scripture and praying the Word with me. On the other hand, the Pastor of the church I was involved in was a little stand offish. Maybe he didn't want to get involved. Maybe he thought I would ask the church for money. Who knows? It really didn't matter. I wasn't seeking any answers from him. He was a very kind man and I had a lot of respect for him. I was just a little taken back by what I perceived as him avoiding any acknowledgment of the mess I was in.

That encouragement I was receiving from Kentucky gave me the courage to seek God with everything I had. I still had the little voice inside my heart saying "I can heal you. All I need is the faith the size of a mustard seed".

I began reading the Bible for hours just looking for some verse to tell me what to do. I would continue walking for miles each day just pouring out my heart to God about my mess.

That television channel I was on was a continuous twenty-four- hour loop filled with three to five minute segments. My face was continuously in that loop. Talk about wearing a mask! I drove around town in my Mercedes being recognized wherever I went. Yet, when I picked up the hometown paper my name was listed in the property section under foreclosures. I may have kept my shame and self-condemnation hid behind my mask but my embarrassment was front and center for the entire town to see.

# 45

## LIGHTEN MY LOAD?—
## PRIORITIZE AND PITCH

Walking and talking with God each day brought more clarity. The little quite voice inside me spoke again. This time He was clearly saying, "Lighten your load". Lighten my load? What could that mean? My load *was* getting lighter. I was losing my house. But strangely, I knew it meant more than that. I knew exactly what those words meant, or so I thought.

It most likely meant I should clean out my closets and get rid of things I really didn't need. Wouldn't that lighten the load of boxes when I left the house? I began tossing clothes and feeling very obedient in the process.

Almost immediately, I got a call from the franchise owner I had worked with in South Carolina. She wanted to ask me some questions about motorcycles. Her nephew was looking to buy one and she wanted my opinion about the safety of certain models. We chatted for a while then I began to tell her my positive experience with my Katana. She said, "Wait, that's a Suzuki, right? I believe that is the one he is interested in." Sure enough, the one he had written down was a Suzuki Katana. I asked her if he had ridden one because the fit of the bike was the most important thing. She said no but that was his favorite motorcycle. I assured her if the bike fit him, he couldn't go wrong. Best of luck to him and I hung up.

As I continued moving my clothes around it was as if God was saying, "AHEM, Lighten Your Load." Oh no, that could not possibly mean my motorcycle? Let's see, it was the middle of winter, I was not looking to sell the bike, and a friend calls out of the blue asking about the exact model sitting in my basement. Okay, I get it! There was no doubt those words *lighten my load* meant more than clothes. Anything but my motorcycle, please!!!

Have you ever had that uncomfortable peace? You know, the very thing you do not want to do is the very thing you know you should do. It is the last thing you would think to do but there is so much peace inside telling you to do it. I could not believe I was going to call her back and tell her I would sell my bike to her nephew. But I did.

The sale of the bike opened my mind to letting go and selling other things I thought I never would. The five- bedroom house had the accumulation of things from my twelve years of marriage and everything I had saved from my childhood. It was time to prioritize and pitch.

I had gone from one extreme to another when it came to pitching. I started thinking I needed to get rid of a few clothes only to end up seeing it as an opportunity to completely make a fresh start. I wasn't sure where I was going but I knew I was leaving the house. What an opportunity to rid myself of memories and junk. I decided that if it had anything to do with my marriage (other than the children) or had anything to do with the relationship with Stefan's father, it was gone!!! I rid myself of everything from tee shirts to furniture. I needed a fresh start in life and that was an excellent opportunity to take it literally.

I was finding freedom watching ties to my past disappear as I pitched. As odd as it seemed, my load was getting lighter. I was eliminating not only my load of stuff but the load of oppression from my past.

Romans 2 "In kindness he takes us firmly by the hand and leads us into a radical life-change."

# 46

## DEBUNK THE LIES—
## JUST TALK TO HIM

I continued to realize that my relationship with God was my only salvation. It wasn't in church activities, Christian television, or even Christian radio. Even though I feel those can be valuable, there comes a point when nothing will satisfy except clear communication with our Creator. I had hit rock bottom but pulled out the stops on seeking Him and Him alone. In addition to prioritizing and pitching my stuff, I prioritized what I was allowing to filter into my thinking.

Waking up in the morning was the worst time of the day. I could not stand the silence. Silence in the room only meant oppressing thoughts were bombarding my brain.

*"There is no reason to get up.... Why should I go on?....I am still alone with people all around me.... This emptiness is going nowhere.... I'd rather sleep than face reality.... I don't want to eat, thinking of food makes me sick.... I'd go back to sleep but I'd just feel all the heaviness when I woke up again.... I hate this sick feeling in my gut.... If I get up, I'm going to throw up.... Why should I pray? God only puts up with me because he is obligated to.... Do I have enough to survive today?... I don't know which is worse, my bad dreams when I am asleep or living this nightmare when I am awake.... I can't sleep but I can't focus either.... I'd rather stay in bed with my thoughts than to get up and live the day."*

Those were only a few of the first thoughts that went through my head as I awoke. It was as if I was back in the Whac A Mole™ game. As soon as I began to wake, the enemy was there with his sack of lies hitting me over the head.

My reaction was to turn on the TV or computer as soon as I began to move. I could fill the room with noise from the TV or radio but it was still very empty. I was so dead inside that I had to begin listening to the Word of God immediately to fight off the oppression. I could easily click on the sermons at victorylifeonline.com and listen to Gary's messages. They were becoming my lifeline of truth. I also had a couple of my favorite Bible teachers I would listen to on television. I had to hear TRUTH for about an hour before I had enough life inside me to face the day.

Why didn't you just sit down with your Bible? You might ask. Sometimes you are in such an intense battle that you need to silence the enemy before you can even think clearly. Sitting silently immediately after I woke up was open ground for the enemy to throw destructive thoughts. I needed someone else fighting that battle with me. That's why I chose to listen to the Word first thing in the morning. I'm sure that is part of the meaning when the Bible says faith comes through hearing and hearing through the word of God.

Spend time listening to an uncompromising teacher. (If you need help identifying one, reach out to me on my website www. Debralynnhayes.com and I will give you the ones I listen to.) God is faithful to his Word. If you give Jesus the slightest consideration, He will reveal Himself and meet you right where you are.

One of the strongest schemes of our enemy is to isolate. He can make you feel you are the only one having those thoughts. You are the only one that has felt that way. And the big lie is: YOU ARE ALONE.

To debunk those lies is easier than you think. If any of them were true they would not have been addressed over two thousand years ago, in the book of James.

"So, let God work his will in you. Yell a loud *no* to the Devil and watch him scamper. Say a quiet *yes* to God and he'll be there in no time. …..Hit bottom, and cry your eyes out…..Get serious, really serious. Get down on your knees before the Master; it's the only way you'll get on your feet."

That my dear friend is the place where healing begins. It is the safe place where you can begin to run toward your pain instead of away from it.

Take control. Start your day with a simple prayer something like this: *God, thank you for giving me this day even though I am struggling for a reason to live it. Jesus, thank you for the abundant life you offer even though it looks like shambles. Holy Spirit, I invite you into this day. Help me to hear with your ears. Help me to see the world through your eyes. Let my heart beat with your heartbeat. Help my feet to walk in the direction you lead. Devil, I will not listen to you and I'm telling you to leave me alone.*

It is very common to approach prayer from the opposite direction. Instead of being honest and admitting we need help, it is often approached as if we're doing God a favor by giving him our time. The key is JUST TALK TO HIM. He likes that. He wants to be your friend not some distant unapproachable figure.

# 47

## GO NORTH—
## YOU'VE BEEN GOING IN
## CIRCLES LONG ENOUGH

I'm sure the neighbors thought I was crazy if they looked out their windows and saw me walking around the neighborhood talking... to God. I became very comfortable chatting with Him and telling Him everything on my heart, good or bad. I also became very acquainted with Him responding. Oh, it was not a verbal response so don't weird out on me. It's that peace that comes when the right thought goes through my mind and I know without a doubt, it's Him leading and directing my life. It's as if the fogs lifts, and I see things clearly.

So, it was, one day as I was walking and talking to God about the uncertainty of moving out of my house. That peace came as the word "GO" went through my head. "Go" was such a generic word. I could easily let my imagination run with it. But I decided to sit tight instead creating my own interpretation.

After my walk, I got on my laptop intending to sit down to a few hours of work. I opened my inbox and there was an email from a Bible teacher that I listened to regularly. The subject line was: GO NORTH. The email quoted a Scripture in Deuteronomy 2. "You have been going around in circles in these hills long enough; go north." Wow, the same peace I felt when I thought the word 'Go' just hit my heart again. I looked up several translations of this verse. Some said hills. Some said mountains but they all basically said one thing. Quit going in circles and Go North.

The email was referring to being in ruts and going in circles in life. But I knew God was saying more to me through this. Still, I waited. The truth was, I had no choice but to wait. If God was telling me to GO, He was going to have to do something like part the Red Sea. I was out of money, I was losing my home, my job was at a dead end and I was not even making enough money to survive. I was going to be at the mercy of family taking me in and God was saying Go North? I didn't even have a family member that lived more North that I could move in with. He certainly could not mean to move out of town. I knew the expenses that would require. Not an Option.

I just let those thoughts go, thinking I was making it up in my head. There is no shame in admitting you missed it. It's all a growing process.

Go North. The second email came the following day. This was a series that Pastor was doing. So, for seven days I got an email saying: Go North.

I told Chris about the emails while we were working. I was laughing about how ridiculous it all sounded. I told him if I WERE to go north I would go to Georgetown or Lexington Kentucky. My heart was attached to the church I had been listening to, but that was crazy thinking because of all the expense it would take to move. Who would rent a place without me having a job? How could I land a job without living there? I was laughing at my desperation.

Nonchalantly, he said, "My brother, who you met in Atlanta, works for a company that is opening an office in Lexington. Do you want me to talk to him?" I gave him one of the looks that a puppy gives when it turns its' head sideways trying to understand what was just said. Of course, talk to him, what could it hurt?

# 48

## LET GO, LET GOD—
## BUT YOU'D BETTER TAKE
## AN AIR MATTRESS

B y then Mom was settled in her new apartment. I had sold
everything possible to give me a little bit of pocket cash.
There was very little movement on potential buyers for the
house.

Worry had attached itself to me and I was beginning to welcome it. Even though I was praying more consistently, *Worrying
Out Loud Is Not Prayer.* I was careful while pouring out my heart
not to be reminding God of every problematic detail like He wasn't
already aware.

Still, I continued to wear my mask proudly. I was the girl on
channel 7 by day and the Worrying Princess by night. At times,
I literally made myself sick worrying. Some days while filming, I
would become so stressed I would throw up. Then immediately
brush my hair, freshen my make up, and go right back in front of
the camera as if my world was one big bouquet of daises.

Chris' brother responded asking for my resume and telling us he
had set up an interview in Lexington. What? Who was I kidding?
I shouldn't even waste their time. Yet, this was one time my mask
was beneficial. I drove straight to Lexington and I interviewed as if
I didn't have a care in the world. When asked if I would be willing
to relocate, I didn't hesitate with my answer 'No Problem!'

I was secretly wishing it were a possibility as I left the interview. However, it had most likely only been a great excuse to get out of town and spend some time with my new friend Tracy. I didn't want to give the impression that I wasted their time in the interview so I stopped at the lab, had the blood work done, and peed in the cup for the employment screening.

I stopped by to see Tracy on my way out of town. She was her consistent faithful self. "Well you never know what God could be up to. We would love you have you with us in Georgetown. Don't limit God. He can work with uncertainty but not unbelief. Give him room to work."

Sure enough. the call came for the second and final interview. Should I or shouldn't I continue playing this game? Where on earth would I live if I continued? I didn't know anyone well enough to think of moving in with them. More importantly, they didn't know me. I was only the girl that drove up occasionally from Tennessee.

Attempting not to limit God, I started looking online for apartments. I saw an ad looking for a female roommate. The ad read: *Looking for roommate to share expenses. Must be clean with a healthy lifestyle, professional, no partying and preferably in their twenties.* I responded right back to the ad: *I am clean and healthy. I am a professional who does not have all night parties. I am not in my twenties but I am pretty cool.* I don't know what I was thinking with that response but I got an immediate return email wanting to chat.

My mask again played in my favor. I didn't reveal any of my problems. I simply told her I was a professional wanting to relocate. I was interviewing for a job in Lexington and was looking at options for limiting expenses during the move. We agreed to talk again after my second interview. When I asked her about the location, I recognized her complex as being the one my junior high sweetheart was living in. I would never want to move beside him and become a nuisance but I did feel a little more secure knowing he would be only a few doors away.

I had not been in contact with him very much through that entire process for three reasons. 1. I wasn't even taking that move seriously myself. 2. If by a longshot, it happened, I would not want him to think I was chasing him or making the move in pursuit of him. 3. I was simply embarrassed of the shape my life was in. I kept thinking, Man, I wish I could have reconnected with him at the height of my life instead of at rock bottom. Who would want someone struggling like I was?

The second interview took place July 28. Within an hour, I was offered the job and told my first day would be Monday, August 8. I quickly made the phone call to the potential roommate from my car. She was willing to take a chance. The room would not be available until Sunday, August 7. I had just enough pocket cash from selling things to send rent for the month of August.

Faith is going to the edge of everything you know and taking one more step.

WOW!!! I believed I had just seen God part the waters for me. In spite, of the fact that I had no money, in spite, of the fact that I only knew two people in Georgetown, in spite, of the fact that I didn't have a job, He completely parted those waters for that move to fall into place. My room was available just one day before my job started. There was no question He made that happen. I could not have orchestrated it if I had wanted to.

On Sunday morning, August 7, 2011, I packed everything I owned into the car. I moved to Kentucky with my clothes in back seat, a borrowed air mattress in the trunk, and my Maggie in the front floor board.

I hadn't met my roommate until the Sunday afternoon when Maggie and I showed up at her door. Tracy was there to take us to dinner as soon as I unloaded my clothes and air mattress. Living with the new roommate turned out to be a blessing. We were different enough in age and interest that there wasn't any drama. She was, no doubt, a God sent.

For the next six months, I slept in the floor on an air mattress because I was half way convinced something would go wrong and I would have to move back.

# 49

## WAS I A FAILURE?—
## IT'S ALL IN HOW YOU LOOK AT IT

I had left the house in the realtors' hands. We had three months to keep it on the market. The second week of August I got a call from a different realtor asking me when I could have my belongings out. She needed to change the locks. After explaining to her that she was obviously mistaken, she informed me that my house had been sold on the court house steps that morning and I no longer owned it.

My realtor was as clueless as I was. Our investigative task resulted in learning that the one department at the bank that was responsible to stop the auction each month had dropped the ball. They had forgotten to contact the third party selling the house that month. Their response was as nonchalant as if they had forgotten a lunch date. No big deal.

It may have been a slight oversight to them but I was devastated. The traffic looking at the house was picking up, then BAM… it was yanked right out from under me. My credit report turned from late payments to foreclosure. I felt like such a failure and was totally embarrassed. Even though it wasn't true, I felt my attempt to settle down there was being laughed at by the whole town. Nothing had worked as I had hoped while moving back to my hometown after so many years.

The lies that I had completely failed were pounding in my head. Relationships had failed. My new career had failed. My attempt to own a home had failed. But the basic truth was this: I had not failed at any of those. The relationship with Stefan's father was something that needed to end. It was toxic. My new career with the TV channel was not a failure. We accomplished everything we had set out to do. We made that new concept a success. The backing for it had simply been misjudged but the task was completely success. I got behind in my mortgage but as the years played out I was compensated a small amount for the illegal way it was taken.

Was I a failure? It is all in how you look at it. I had made some bad choices which led to some sticky situations. Did that make me a failure? No. However, when I left town I had not realized that. I saw myself as a huge failure. Even though I had just made what was perceived by some to be a courageous move, I lived each day with a complete attitude of survival.

I faced my new opportunity in Kentucky with a defeated mind set. I had it all, lost it all, then realized I didn't need it all. Where does a person go from there? Unfortunately, I developed the attitude that if I didn't have anything, I wouldn't have to go through the pain of losing it. Where I had been a driven independent person, in my mind I had become a grasshopper. Where my mind had always looked to the future, I only looked paycheck to paycheck to survive.

It was difficult getting on my feet in Kentucky. The transitional job I took to move wasn't the best fit. I was confined to a cubicle. For years, I worked in three countries. Spending hours upon hours each day in a 3' x 3' space was very uncomfortable. I was thankful for that initial job but I jumped at a different opportunity when it came along.

The new opportunity put me back into the community. The base pay was very minimal for the first year but there was promise for future growth. It was in the wellness field and I looked forward to the education I would receive during that first year. The corporate office was in Chicago so frequent visits put me back in touch with my friends who lived there. If I could survive that first year of minimal pay it could be very fulfilling.

I survived but my pride did not. I learned how to stretch a dollar in so many ways it became distorted. I learned to do without things that were not a necessity. I even learned to do without things that were necessities. One week I was completely without food and toilet paper for four days. I drank lots of water to stay hydrated and managed to make two very small protein shakes. If Jesus had done it for forty days, surely, I would survive four. The difference was, He was led to do it.

You know you are dealing with your pride when you would rather use a wash cloth and wash it out each time you went to the toilet than to let anyone know you needed toilet paper. Fortunately, when you aren't eating you don't go to the bathroom as much. (I threw that rag away as soon as I got my next check...)

Tracy and Gary had given me gift cards to help with food and gas when I initially moved to Kentucky. But six months had passed and I had changed jobs. I was too prideful to let anyone know I needed food. I didn't want to be perceived as the new girl who was always asking for help.

I know if I had asked the church they would have gotten food or a family in the church would have stepped in and asked me to come to their house to eat. I know if I had told my junior high sweetheart that I needed food, he would have taken me to the grocery store. The only thing stopping me was my pride. Therefore, my pride and I sat and suffered for four days. When the check finally came, it was as if God said, "Well, aren't you proud of yourself? Now, let's talk about that pride."

It is easier for me to be a giver than a receiver. If I knew of anyone trying to work but having a hard time, I would not hesitate at all to lend a hand with what I had. Why did I not think other people would feel the same way? I suffered unnecessarily and most likely robbed someone else of feeling the satisfaction of being a blessing. Pride is an ugly thing and offers no benefits whatsoever.

# 50

## FIND YOUR DIRT—
## AND YOU WILL GROW

When a palm tree is planted in Michigan, it struggles to grow. It constantly needs nurturing. It fights to survive because the environment isn't right. The only chance to live is if artificial surroundings are provided. We have all seen indoor pools at hotels where one solitary palm tree is planted to create atmosphere. It is living but not thriving. If one element of that environment changed the palm tree would die instantly. It is artificially created for appearance.

If that same palm tree is planted in sunny Florida it will flourish on its own simply because it is in the environment where it was created to be. When that tree is rooted in the correct dirt it can stand even hurricane sized storms.

The same thoughts can be applied when it comes to finding the correct church. You will know when you fit. There is an element of *real* all around you. Nothing artificial needs to sustain you. We were very fortunate that we found our dirt, so to speak, while living in Ohio. Even though the storms we faced there were monumental, we were rooted.

The move to Kentucky was simply because I recognized my *dirt* and knew I needed to plant myself there to grow. I had no idea of the clarity that was waiting and the healing I would experience. God oftentimes leads us with a nudge instead of painting the full picture. I know for me, if I had the full picture, I would probably mess up the plan trying to make it happen on my own. God shows us a little bit at a time, and if we continue to follow, it leads to much more than we could imagine.

How do you recognize your *dirt* when looking for a church? First, you have it all backwards if you are looking for the church to be your answer. There is a verse in the Bible that says if you seek HIM you **will** find Him. Regardless of how much seeking you are doing, if you open the door the least little bit, He will show up. The answer will be in a relationship with Jesus not in church activities. The activities will only enhance and fulfill what is already in your heart. I recognized my dirt in Kentucky when I listened to the sermons online. I was hearing the exact same thing that was in my heart as I spent time in the Word. Some call it confirmation.

I was desperately seeking answers. I was tired of Sunday morning routines that never changed. I was tired of never really seeing lives transformed. I was tired of showing up each Sunday and feeling everyone had their life together but me. I was tired of leaving the building feeling like I had put on a nice plastic performance, but my heart was still aching.

I knew other people had to be facing messy lives like mine. Why did those messes always need to be hidden at church? Wasn't that the place where hope should be found? Why do people feel inferior to admit they don't have it all together? Why was Sunday church such a separate thing than Monday thru Saturday life? Even with Christian radio…why weren't the songs I listened to during the week, that were so inspirational to me, ever played on Sunday? Wasn't God the same Sunday thru Sunday? Wasn't He with us every day? Why did we make that one hour on Sunday so superficial?

I knew I had found my dirt the first Easter Sunday I attended Victory Life. The room was packed. The lights were low. The video started on the big screens. There were clips of the Crucifixion from the movie "*The Passion*".[1] The scenes of the pain Jesus endured were hard to watch. The music accompanying the video was "*Hero*"[2] by *Skillet*. I looked around and there wasn't a dry eye in the room. Teenagers to people in their elder years were intently watching and being touch by the reality of what Easter meant. They were seeing who Jesus was and not just the religious idea.

I did not see any religious walls. There were no age barriers. There were no religious traditions that said, "We can't do that, we've never done it that way before." There were no musical barriers. (When you have people in their 80's crying to *Skillet* you know that the Truth has broken through).

The heart of the Pastor sets the tone. Gary had grown up in drugs and was an alcoholic before meeting Jesus. After his life was changed, his heart remained to reach the people who were caught in those same traps. The atmosphere had adapted to our culture without compromising the message. The mission God had given him was to reach the unchurched people and the ones with a bad taste in their mouth about church and God.

The congregation does not hear religious phrases just to smooth the conscience. They get a very bold, direct and challenging message. Because there is understanding and no condemnation coming from the pulpit, people feel the freedom to be exposed with whatever they're dealing with. That kind of freedom ushers in genuine relationships. People tend to give others the benefit of doubt they give themselves. There seems to always be someone dealing with something you can help with. There also seems to be someone who has been where you are and can offer help to you. Those relationships seem to flourish when Jesus is kept in the center. It truly was a place to grow instead of pretend. I don't want to paint a picture of perfection. Anytime a group of people try to work together, issues arise. But when we embrace the verse that iron sharpens iron so one person sharpens another, growth can be a beautiful thing.

Gary will be the first one to tell a visitor if our style is not for them he will certainly help them find a church where the Word is not compromised and may be a better fit. Just as the palm tree thrives in Florida but struggles in Michigan, Oak trees do better in Michigan than Florida. It is important to find YOUR dirt. A sincere pastor will realize that and be willing to help you locate your dirt.

I will always be thankful that God used a friend I met when I was twelve to open the door to Kentucky. I will always feel honored that a stranger named Tracy showed the love of God to me. I will always stand amazed how God works through such a unique group of people. I often describe the relationships I made after I moved to Kentucky as a bouquet of wildflowers. Nothing is exactly perfect or perfectly arranged, but together it is beautiful. At Victory Life Church, I simply found a group of imperfect people who love the Lord and love each other.

# 51

## OWN IT—
## AND LET IT GO

My roots were growing deep into Kentucky dirt. Week after week the words of Truth infused into the layers of the guilt and self- condemnation I had carried for years. The longer you carry a weight the heavier it becomes.

My mask was still secure but I was beginning to allow thoughts to reach into my heart which addressed the abortion of Stefan. Why was that guilt so hard? I wasn't unfamiliar with God's forgiveness. I certainly was comfortable asking forgiveness when I had a misunderstanding with someone. I had no problem forgiving someone when they brought issues to me. Why was I still tripping? I had taken my share of the responsibility for that decision. I knew I would always feel regret, but was I completely convinced that I shouldn't carry the shame with me all my life? Was I sure God didn't take Ephraim and Isaac and Randall to get back at me?

Month after month of being around the uncompromised Word of God brought the same words. "I refuse to blame God." Over and over through the sermons I heard, "I refuse to blame God." Could I say with certainty that I didn't blame God? How many things in my life and in the world in general did I really blame God for? I began to realize that my deep- rooted problem was not the guilt I was carrying but my view of who God was. When did I accept the lie that God was against me and not for me? Where did I pick up the image that God was mad at me and just waiting for an opportunity to get me?

Instead of those lies repeating in my head I was now hearing:

I John 3:20 "God is greater than our worried hearts. He knows more about us than we know ourselves. And friends, once that is taken care of and we are no longer accusing or condemning ourselves, we're bold and free before God. We're able to stretch our hands out and receive what we asked for because we're doing what he said, doing what pleases him".

I John 3:20 NKJV "For if our heart condemns us, God is greater than our heart and knows all things."

Isaiah 60 "I will be your eternal light. Your days of grieving are over"

Jeremiah 29:11 "I know what I am doing. I have it all planned out-plans to take care of you, not abandon you, plans to give you the future you hope for."

Jeremiah 29:11 NKJV "For I know the plans I have for you, says the Lord, they are plans for good and not for disaster, to give you a future and a hope"

Ephesians 1 "Because of the sacrifice of the Messiah, his blood poured out on the altar of the Cross, we're a free people-free of penalties and punishments chalked up by all our misdeeds. And not just barely free, either. *Abundantly* free!" Ephesians 1

When the truth of who God really is, was spoken week after week the lies I believed exposed themselves. I had finally decided to move toward all the pain I was carrying instead of away from it. What I found was that I had nothing to fear. The lies I believed of who God was had kept me trapped. I had trusted him with my move to Kentucky but not my deepest pain. Not the one I kept hidden. Not the one I didn't want to admit. When I began to understand just how good He is I began taking off my mask to deal with the abortion.

I had finally removed my mask and was looking myself squarely in the mirror. I had to admit the truth to myself. Ironically, my mask was only hiding me from me. I would not be able to let go of that guilt until I was ready to own it.

Yes! I had decided to stop the life of my baby. Yes! That abortion could have been partly responsible for the future complications in pregnancies. Yes! I was the one who followed someone who was running *from* the pregnancy. Yes! It was ME that changed my life forever. IT WAS ME!!!!

I felt safe enough to completely let go once I saw God as the best friend I could run to. That is the beauty of salvation. I could break down and sob for my own actions knowing I was in loving arms. They were not the same tears of built up grief I had cried before. Those were humble tears of remorse. I knew I could let go of all the weight and still be fully accepted. I didn't have to be my own physician any longer. I could genuinely bring my guilt to Him and know I could walk away without it.

I know these words sound trite and religious to a point, but let me paint another picture. Imagine someone you trust and feel very secure with. You bury your head in their shoulder and cry your eyes out with your deepest pain. At the point where there are no more tears, that person puts their arm around you and holds you tight and begins to walk with you saying," It's okay. It's all over. Your future is bright. I have made some plans that are going to make you feel so much better. Come with me, let me show you."

The hardest guilt to let go of is the one you can do nothing about. It may be words of regret to someone who has passed. It may be words you never said to someone who has passed. It may be a baby you can't get back.

There is a sense of control when we can do something about the guilt we feel. Maybe we talk to someone and ask forgiveness. Maybe we write a letter. Maybe we decide to remain stubborn and carry the guilt. The control remains our own. But when you do not want to carry the guilt and there is no earthly way to get rid of it, you must know that you can safely take it to Jesus. You will walk away knowing that it's okay. You will feel a freedom and hope you never imagined.

# 52

# THE ROAD—
# TO RISE

I hope you found inspiration and encouragement in the exposure of my life. I'd love to say that Part Three ended with my knight in shining armor sweeping me off my feet and we loved happily ever after. But that didn't happen. Who knows? It still may. I'd love to say that somehow children were restored to my life and I had babies to hold and love. But that didn't happen. Who knows? It still may. I'd love to say I had another house and it was paid for. But that didn't happen. Who knows? It still may. What I can say is that I learned to be totally fulfilled right where I am.

If anyone looked at my life the moment I finished writing this book, it would not be the fairy tale ending people dream of. Life isn't about fairy tales. It is about reality and knowing that our circumstances do not define us. The more I learned about my heavenly father, the more He defined me. I separated the things I had done from who I was.

I no longer see lack in my life. I no longer see despair and disappointment. I see promise and excitement. I'm just waiting to see what's going to happen next.

I'M NOT DEAD AND GOD'S NOT DONE!!!

I choose to believe this: Isaiah 58 "I will always show you where to go. I'll give you a full life in the emptiest of places – firm muscles, strong bones. You'll be like a well-watered garden, a gurgling spring that never runs dry."

I want to encourage everyone. **There is hope**. It may simply be something as disappointing as my derailed weekend meeting Kevin Costner, a broken relationship that leaves your heart and your life empty or a tragedy that has left you in shock. Regardless of what you are facing, the four steps I share in Part Four can be applied to your life and you too will **RISE**. Let God define who you are, not your circumstances.

# PART FOUR

## RISE

*"You heal these wounds;*
*Unseal my tomb;*
*And I'll* **RISE** *Undefeated!!!"*

Collin Raye. 'Undefeated'

R - RELATIONSHIP NOT RELIGION

I – INTENTIONAL LIVING

S – SCRIPTURE FOR THE MOMENT

E – ETERNITY

# R
## RELATIONSHIP NOT RELIGION

PSALM 71 "I run for dear life to God, I'll never live to regret it. Do what you do so well: get me out of this mess and up on my feet."

Let me begin this section by saying that this will not be easy but, oh, it will be worth it.

Many people try to find answers and healing in traditional forms of religion. Anything short of a relationship with God leaves you open for disappointment. It is very simple. An intimate relationship with God can bring the desired healing.

The words *relationship with God* have become very trite in our society. Many people have mistaken going through religious activities as a "relationship." Religion can end up hurting you or keeping you shielded from knowing the only one who knows you inside out. I can promise, if you look for deep comfort in religion, your emotions will become shredded.

Unfortunately, what the world labels as religion reflects the attitude: if you come to our group, sing our music, dress like us, act like us then we will accept you. It is often self- based and full of judgement.

Jesus defines religion quite differently in James when He says real religion is reaching out to the homeless, widows and orphans.

Relationship says in John 3 "This is how much God loved the world: that he gave his son, his one and only son. And this is why: so that no one need be destroyed! By believing in him, anyone can have a whole and lasting life. God didn't go to all the trouble of sending his Son merely to point an accusing finger, telling the world how bad it was."

Let's not confuse the terms religion and church. In their truest forms, they both have a positive meaning. Religion is helping others. Church is the people doing the helping, not a place with four walls. The enemy has twisted these terms in our society. Today those terms are interpreted to mean a schedule of activities done on Sunday morning at a place called Church. Moving forward in this section, I am saying that it is intimacy with God himself that brings healing. (That is Relationship) It is not the schedule of activities done on Sunday at a place we call Church. (That is Religion)

Many people who gather in "church" have the purest hearts you will find while many are filled with judgement. Many people who do not gather in "church" have a true relationship with God while many do not have clue who he is. That is why the Bible says God looks at the heart of a man.

When God looks at us He doesn't go through our behavior checklist. He sees us as family. He accepts us exactly where we are. Many times, when I have felt like such a failure I could almost feel Him hugging me and saying, "Come on, we will work on it together." That is my prayer: that you can get past your wounds to feel His hugs and know He is on your side. He is indeed willing to jump into your life right where you are.

Life leaves us scarred from pain and disappointment. It is not uncommon for those scars to become a large part of our identity. We feel very threatened to let anyone close to them, especially a God who is often blamed for the scars in the first place. The biggest deception of the enemy is blaming a loving God, when he himself is the one with the agenda to steal, kill and destroy. That is the first lie to be debunked in the process of intimacy with God. The first step to debunking that lie is just talking to God and not holding anything back. He can take whatever ever you want to say and you will be surprised how he responds with love.

I know. It is extremely hard to begin those conversations. It is not easy but it is SO worth it. Maybe you don't know what to say or maybe you have repeated the same words in prayer for so long it is hard to change. Maybe you are ashamed of the first thoughts that go through your head as you become quiet. That quiet moment is when Religion whispers, "You should not feel that way. Who do you think you are?" Upon thinking that, it is easy to jump over into plastic performance or give up on talking to Him altogether.

What do I mean by *plastic performance prayers*? That is having a conversation with God where all the words coming out of your mouth are proper and polite while the thoughts going through your head are a different story.

If you do not get anything else out of this book: **GET THIS.** It is okay to feel how you are feeling. There is no shame or condemnation. You are fully accepted. Your journey to abundance with God can only begin right where you are. Just talk to Him. Be clear about this. *Whatever you are feeling right now, it is OKAY to feel that way.*

I am sure several people reading this have been through their own hell. Pain comes in various ways to different people. No ones' pain should be measured against anyone else's. Everyone has different trigger points that stir up the emotions attached to wounds. The easiest thing to do with those emotions is hold them inside. Emotions were made to give away. The question is who can we trust to give them to? The answer is to start with God.

Before you close this book and walk away please realize if someone had told me *just give it to God* in the middle of my depression I would have probably thrown something at them. God was the last person I wanted to try to talk to. Usually the people we run from are the very ones who have something we desperately need. It is true with God also. Just give Him a chance to prove Himself. We have a perfect example to follow.

Most people have heard of King David in the Bible. Some people are aware that God called him a man after his own heart. But few people pay attention to the Psalms he wrote which are called the Imprecatory Psalms. We can see in the Imprecatory Psalms that a soul needs the expression as much as it needs the answer.

"According to Theopedia, an encyclopedia of Christianity, the imprecatory Psalms contain curses or prayers for the punishment of the psalmist's enemies. To imprecate means 'to invoke evil upon, or curse.'

These Psalms are written by David, a king of Israel, someone the Bible identifies as a man after God's own heart (see Acts 13:22). The Bible holds up David as an example to emulate.

Because the Bible gave him this label, you might think his psalms would be sanitized and pain-free. A few might match that description, but certainly not the imprecatory ones. These ancient writings are chock-full of struggle, tension, doubt, anger, revenge, hurt, and fear."

Before we look at some of those Imprecatory Psalms let's look at Psalm 37. This verse shows that David was a man who continually communicated with God. First, he would never be able to be so bold if he didn't fully trust God to accept him the way he was at that moment. The text also exemplifies probably the most important rule for any relationship, especially one with God. *He talked to **God** about his feelings.* He did not run to other people. Granted in David's case, his two choices to talk to were usually only God and sheep. We honestly should view our choices as the same. Talk to God or talk to sheep (other people). Sure, there are times to get counsel from others. That should be done after time is spent talking to God. Then only with people who have a sincere desire to help move you forward not just to talk in circles.

David gives us instruction in Psalm 37 to be bold and honest when we talk to God. After being bold and honest, expect him to take care of things.

PSALM 37 "Open up before God…. Hold nothing back……. He'll do whatever needs to be done!"

Maybe God saw David as a man after his own heart because he held nothing back. With any relationship, the more vulnerable we make ourselves the more intimacy can come.

Humans let us down. We are all human and hurt each other unintentionally and sometimes intentionally every day. The results often cause us to build walls around our hearts. These walls remain as we approach God. We expect to receive the same treatment from

Him. It is scary to begin thinking about taking down those walls and becoming vulnerable as we talk to Him.

You might even think, "How can I trust a God I am so angry with?" Just admit the anger and talk to Him anyway. Hold nothing back. We fear His wrath but hope for His grace. I can promise you from my experience, you will find His grace!!!

Following David's expressions in the Psalms gives us a perfect example of holding nothing back.

Let's look at some of his cries of **frustration**:

PSALM 10 "God are you avoiding me? Where are you when I need you?"

PSALM 6 "Please God, not more yelling, No more trips to the wood shed: Treat me nice for a change: Can't you see I'm black and blue, beat up badly in bones and soul? God how long will it take for you to let up?"

PSALM 40 "Now God, don't hold out on me. Don't hold back your passion. Soften up God and intervene, hurry and get me some help."

PSALM 35 "My prayers were like lead in my gut"

This is what he says when he feels like he is in **trouble**.....Take time to read Psalm 69 and 70 from beginning to end. This is a taste of what you will find.

PSALM 69 "God, God save me. I'm in over my head. Don't look the other way, your servant can't take it. I'm in trouble... Answer right now!"

"I yell out to My God, I yell with all my might. I yell at the top of my lungs, He Listens"

PSALM 70 "But I've lost it. I'm wasted. God----quickly, quickly! Quick to my side, quick to my rescue! God, don't lose a minute."

Then there are times of **boldness** when he is talking to God about his anger toward his enemies.

PSALM 56 "Pay them back in Evil...Get angry God!!!! Down with these People!!"

PSALM 58 "God Smash their teeth to bits......Leave them toothless tigers.... Let their lives be buckets of water spilled. All that's left is a damp stain in the sand"

PSALM 69 "Make them become blind as bats, Give them the shakes from morning to night. Let them know what you think of them. Blast them with your red- hot anger."

Wow, I don't know about you, but I'd feel uncomfortable saying all those things to God. We know in the New Testament we are told to pray for our enemies. I'm not so sure those are the words God had in mind when he instructed us to do that. What we can learn is that David fully trusted God with his heart. I'm sure the beautiful songs of worship and praise that David wrote came after his boldness as he brought his raw emotions to God.

The one I personally related to the most was when David was feeling **embarrassment.** That is exactly how I felt after Isaac was born then went immediately to Heaven. I felt like God had played a trick on me by letting me get pregnant again, only to see another baby go to Heaven. I found some comfort in knowing that a person after God's own heart shared my same thoughts in Psalm 69.

PSALM 69 "Because of you I look like an idiot, I walk around ashamed to show my face."

There is an old saying that you can't steer a parked car. I believe this holds true in our relationship and communication with God. He can't direct our life to the abundance he wants for us while our prayers are parked behind plastic. It must start exactly where we are with our raw feelings. God can then begin to steer and direct us toward our healing and the plans HE has.

If you read my story in this book you know my intimate relationship with God began with my prayer, "I can't trust my husband and I don't even like you anymore." He immediately answered with love and my healing began. It did not happen overnight. Many times, I got distracted in the process. But thankfully step by step I continued and layer by layer the wounds were healed.

There are now three prayers I pray regularly. I am not in any way arrogant enough to believe I have the edge on praying. I only share with you the three prayers that guide my life knowing God will give personal prayers for your life.

*Prayer 1: Holy Spirit I invite you into my day. Please lead me and guide me through each step. Give me your eyes so I can see the world the way you do. Give me your ears so I can hear people's heart and not their words. Let my heart beat with your heartbeat so I will lean toward compassion instead of judgement. Help my feet to follow so I will be in step with your directions instead of the routines of my day.*

*Prayer 2: Jesus please close the wrong doors in my life so tight I could not push them open if I wanted to. Please swing open the right doors so widely I cannot miss them. I refuse to live in confusion.*

*Prayer 3: Jesus, I take my thoughts captive to your thoughts. I will stay in your Word looking for direction. Bring your Words to my mind exactly when I need them. Please take any of my thoughts that are my own vain imaginations and squash them. But please feed and water any dreams you have put in my heart that are indeed from you and bigger than I will allow myself to think.*

Do I live a flawless life? Absolutely NOT!! Do I miss it daily with my quick attitudes? YES. Have I seen change and progress in myself since I began praying those prayers regularly? ABSOLUTELY. Life is a journey and growth is the reward.

A dear friend of mine once said, "Your opinion of God will determine what you will receive from God."[1] Our opinion of God is usually warped by the lies of the enemy. Therefore, when we approach Him in prayer we are not positioned to receive all He wants to give. It is perfectly okay to begin small when learning to open- up to Him. You will find He is trustworthy and has no intention to harm or ignore you.

PSALM 34 "Look at Him, give Him your warmest smile. Never hide your feelings from Him."

Every relationship we are involved in requires a degree of vulnerability, effort, and honesty. The amount of these three that we put into any relationship will determine the outcome. The same is true with our relationship with God. It is the same but altogether different. God is perfect and constant yet never interfering. He understands us through and through. Fortunately, we do not have to stress about the way we communicate with Him because He already knows every emotion going on inside us. We come to many realizations about ourselves as we continue talking with Him. This is where He can begin or continue the deep healing we need.

It is true that most of us approach God the same way we approach our relationships with other people. We all have layers of pride, fear of rejection, the need for approval, inferiority, and a biggie called unworthiness through false humility. We bring these into our communication with God. Without taking off in a totally different direction here, there is a lot of truth in the fact that the way we relate to our earthly fathers is oftentimes the same place we begin our communication with God. Sometimes that is good and sometimes that is not so good.

For me, I grew up with a lot of fun and openness with Daddy. Yet, he was a workaholic and rarely home. I knew without a doubt that he loved me but there was a constant battle for his attention. As you have read in earlier chapters, when I played basketball I did not doubt that Daddy would be there. Therefore, I became very performance oriented.

That carried over into the early years of my relationship with God. I think I did everything there was to do at a Baptist Church except sing. Come to think of it, I even attempted that though I am NOT a singer. The congregation was very gracious to let me "sing unto the Lord." (While it's true that everyone should raise their voice in praise it was obvious not everyone should have a microphone while doing it.) I found my musical offering on the keyboard. I played the piano every Sunday. In my mind, the more I could do, the more God was pleased with me. I taught Sunday School Classes. I was heavily involved in a youth group. I went on mission trips. I did visitations, home bible studies and prayer groups. I helped with Valentines Banquets and other fun related parties. I was involved in fund raisers for worthy causes. The only thing left to do in the Baptist world was go to seminary and become a preacher. If women preachers hadn't been frowned upon at that time, I probably would have done that too.

While Psalm 51 clearly says, "Going through the motions doesn't please you, a flawless performance is nothing to you", let me insert here that there is nothing at all wrong with serving in your local church. In fact, the more our love for the Lord grows the more we will want to serve Him by serving others. Serving in the local church should come as an expression of our love for the Lord not an effort to gain His approval.

When the storms of life hit and I had to say good bye to my children, nothing I had done *for God* brought any comfort. There was nothing I could *do* at that point to feel close to God or feel He was on my side. I had carried the responsibility to perform for God for so long I did not know how to rest in his love. I did not know the intimacy with Him that is beyond anything that could be shared with another human. Sure, I had been in meetings where lots of emotions were stirred up. I had been in the presence of the Lord through music, worship and even prophetic words. None of that even begins to compare with that sweet spot of communication with God. That place where you have His full attention and He totally understands everything about you. In that sweet spot, there is no condemnation. You have complete acceptance. You can be who you are, where you are. You can become all He made you to be and have the freedom to make mistakes in the process.

Maybe it is my background and the years I have spent in sales, marketing and negotiations but I believe that the way to get to the true heart of something is to peel back the layers that do not belong. I am going to touch on a few of the barriers to that sweet intimacy with God. This is in no way an inclusive list.

If we begin to listen to our prayers (or lack thereof) we can begin to hear our own barriers of communication with Him.

1. Lies and Fear of Rejection ......It is hard not to put these two together. I believe they go hand in hand. This one has the potential of causing the most negative ripples in our life if we do not get anchored in communication with God. We have all known someone, or maybe we are that person, who will say whatever they think the person they are talking to wants to hear. They will say whatever is necessary to keep from hurting or disappointing the other person. In a twisted way, they think they are doing a good thing. In all honesty, they are only being selfish to protect their own heart from being rejected. They end up hurting the other

person worse than the truth ever would have. They may think the other person is too weak to handle the truth. The people they are close to eventually begin to doubt everything they say. Words have no value and the only thing consistent in that relationship is inconsistency and lies. Because of the fear, lying becomes a habit. They aren't even aware of their own transparency. The sad thing is they end up getting the result they were trying so desperately to avoid. They are trapped in their lies and end up losing. The relationship is so damaged with trust issues that it is a constant struggle of ups and downs.

On the other side of the coin, most of us have known people like that and have had to make a conscience choice to keep them in our lives or cut the ties. The easiest thing is to cut the ties and walk away. However, because of connections, that is sometimes not an option. Other times we choose to keep them in our lives because we sincerely love them. We hope and pray one day they realize they don't need to lie to remain accepted. Unfortunately, the relationship becomes more surface and shallow over time because there is no trust.

Jesus gives us several examples of speaking the truth in love. Sometimes the truth may be hard to hear, but in the end, it will bring the clarity we are all searching for.

The lies and fear of rejection can be the biggest barrier to not holding anything back when talking to God. We fear condemnation and judgement. It all comes down to trusting Him with our truth. We need to learn to pour our hearts out and find the acceptance with the one who made us. Our relationships will then find honesty and transparency. It may be hard at first but as we begin to pull back the layers of our hearts or pull off our mask, we WILL find grace, acceptance and a love we have never experienced. Once a person has confidence in being bold and not holding anything back from God, they find the confidence to speak truth in other relationships.

2. Pride and Inferiority - These are two more opposites that go hand in hand. We all know people who we don't want to be around because they always "one up" us. They have bigger or better. They have been more places and have had more experiences. The most common is that no matter where the conversation goes, they "know" more about the topic than anyone else. After a while, we simply tune that person out. Unfortunately, their need to impress is a cover up for an area in their life where they feel very insecure or inferior. That is such a fine line. Their need to impress and gain approval is often the very thing that causes people to reject them.

   When it comes to our level of intimacy with God, pride and inferiority are hard ones to overcome. How can anyone begin to impress the one who made everything and gave us breath? This type of person is usually more comfortable praying out loud and in front of people than having a one on one conversation with God. These prayers tend to sound more like a list of accomplishments we need to remind God of. When I hear prayers like this, I can almost hear God saying "If you can't talk TO me, please don't talk AT me." The first step to healing is letting that pride and inferiority become vulnerable to the Holy Spirit.

3. Performance Orientation, Unworthiness and False Humility – It may be a little tougher to see how these three tie together but hang with me as I walk you through them. We have already touched on the perceived need to perform to please God. Could we gain anymore of His love from anything we DO? There is no question of His love. The question becomes: how much of His love do we allow? He is willing to get involved in our lives only to the degree we allow. He will never disrespect our will.

   Unworthiness is form of shame. After reading my story about my abortion of Stefan, you saw how the shame I lived with was also a driving force in my life. Even though I usually over performed in business I felt unworthy of any award I achieved. Therefore, I accepted them with false humility.

When you are in this mindset you live with the inner struggle that you are never enough. Those thoughts played out in my life for years. I was always outperforming in my career, yet when it came to personal relationships I always felt I never measured up. I felt I was never enough for the person who had earned my interest.

My prayer life was very aggressive for other people. I was bold going to God on their behalf. When it came to praying for myself, I prayed with the attitude of the grasshopper. I never felt I deserved anything and that God was rolling His eyes as I prayed for me.

As with anything you must start right where you are. *Just Talk To Him.* I promise He will not disappointment you. The key is DO NOT GIVE UP. Even if you think the answers you are looking for do not come in the time frame you think they should. DO NOT GIVE UP. As with any relationship, Trust comes with Time.

Resist the temptation to act like it doesn't hurt. You must let it hurt to get to the other side of the pain. You can see in my story it was a few years after the children went to Heaven before I finally let it hurt. The day I misplaced Buster triggered that untouched wound. Up until then, I managed to hold the pain inside. When I finally allowed myself to let it hurt, I was ready to receive the deeper healing and move toward my abundant life.

God waits for us to come to Him with that pain. The deeper the communication you have with Him about the pain the more of the abundance you can receive. It's like pouring dirty water out of a container to receive the fresh. It can be done a little at a time or all at once. As you pour fresh water in to a pail of dirty water, it will eventually force the dirty out. Or you can completely dump the dirty water out at one time and have a clean empty pail ready to receive pure and fresh water. It is the same with our heart. Go ahead and let it hurt and dump out the pain. You will not remain empty. God is ready and waiting to fill you with fresh comfort, hope and abundance.

PSALM 56 TLB "You keep track of all my sorrows. You have collected all my tears in your bottle."

PSALM 34 "If your heart is broken, you'll find God right there; if you're kicked in the gut, he'll help you catch your breath".

I personally think one of the biggest mistakes Christians make is setting up camp, so to speak, on the road to the abundant life God has for them. Always be grateful for the people and situations God uses to move you from one place to another in your journey, but never put more focus on them than Him. Keep God first in your thoughts so you are open to hear the next steps He has for you.

I used to think abundance meant you had everything you needed and enough left over to help someone else. I now know that abundance means the freedom you have inside your heart when you literally embrace the adventurous ride God has planned for you. Abundance is a lifestyle... not a net worth.

The Bible tells us to seek Him first and all the material things we need will come. Once again, the deceptive enemy has twisted that around. If he can get us to believe that abundance is primarily material possessions, then we will seek them first. Our goal becomes striving to achieve. We think if we achieve a certain level, we can call ourselves *blessed by God.*

The truth is just the opposite. If we seek blessings from God FIRST, as in *The Prayer of Jabez,* life becomes an adventure. Everything inside us becomes content looking forward to whatever is around the next corner. We may not know what that is but we know and trust the one leading us. There is a certain excitement we wake up with as we face each day. Our worry is not about survival or building material wealth. Our thoughts shift to praying we can stay healthy and enjoy anything life offers.

I think too that when most Christians read John 10:10 and it talks about abundant life, they relate it to a future time when they get to Heaven. I believe most Christians begin on the road to this abundant life but they stop somewhere along the way. Comfort is often confused with achievement. In Ephesians, the Bible says He is able to do all we could ask or think. I love the way the Message says it, "God can do anything, you know – far more than you could ever imagine or guess or request in your wildest dreams! He does it not by pushing us around but by working within us, his Spirit deeply and gently within us." What would happen in our lives if we continued to imagine, guess or request from God once we had reached our comfort levels?

Comfort zones are where religion begins to set in and relationship begins to dwindle. Religion and Routine versus Relationship and Reality. Religion and routine can always bring us to our comfort zones. I dare say we can achieve that on our own quite effortlessly. But when we have that intimate communication with God, He never lets us get too comfortable. He is always up for another ride. Sometimes He lets us in on where that ride is heading and sometimes He only describes it step by step. But either way, it is an adventure!

PSALM 91 "If you'll hold on to me for dear life," says God, "I'll get you out of any trouble, I'll give you the best of care. If you'll only get to know and trust me, Call me and I'll answer, be at your side in bad times. I'll rescue you, then throw you a party. I'll give you a long life, give you a long drink of salvation!"

JOB 5:9 "After all, he's famous for great and unexpected acts: There is no end to His Surprises."

## THOUGHTS AND DISCUSSION QUESTIONS:

1. What is YOUR opinion of God? (Do not use any religious or church words)

_____

_____

_____

_____

_____

_____

_____

2. What is GODS' opinion of you? (Find Scripture to back it up)

_____

_____

_____

_____

_____

_____

_____

3. Can you identify any barriers to your prayers?

_____

_____

_____

_____

_____

_____

4. Are there any comfort levels in your life where you have stopped seeking God? If so, can you identify why? (ex. Got too busy … too much pain)

_____

_____

_____

_____

_____

_____

_____

5. If you were to ask God for your wildest dream, what would it be?

_____

_____

_____

_____

_____

_____

_____

# I

## INTENTIONAL LIVING

To RISE is a choice. To RISE begins with being intentional. To RISE we must be on purpose. The easiest thing to do is always the easiest thing not to do. Therefore, it is easy to get caught in a trap or rut after a disappointment or personal tragedy. The enemy would like nothing better than to keep us stuck. Our lives go in circles, both mentally and physically, if we listen to him. We may not know exactly where we are headed but one thing is certain: We cannot move toward our healing and abundant living without taking that first step.

You may be familiar with the Bible story about the Israelites when they left Egypt. Or you may have seen the powerful Moses scene, in the movie *The Ten Commandments*, when God parted the Red Sea. Did you notice that the sea did not begin to part until they put their foot in the water? It is the same with our healing. One intentional step begins the process. Intentional actions keep the journey going.

Intentional living is an ongoing process. Some days are perfect and some days seem like you've fallen backwards a few steps. That's okay! You will see progress, if you continue making strides.

Let's look again at John 10:10. AMP "The thief comes only in order to steal and kill and destroy. I came that they may have and enjoy life, and have it in abundance [to the full, till it overflows]. I believe the most important word in that Scripture is AND. Have **and** enjoy life, **and** have it in abundance.... Jesus did not say he died to give us abundant life providing nothing terrible happens in our lives. He expected life to hit us **and** hit us hard. He made the way to enjoy life **and** have a full life regardless of the terrible things the enemy throws at us.

I know that all sounds great in theory but how do we tap into that abundant life? Do we sit and wait for it to come upon us like sunshine hits our face after a cloud rolls away? Abundance doesn't come as a reward or consolation prize for a trial or battle we have endured. It is a mind set and lifestyle learned through the process.

We must make an intentional effort to enjoy that abundant mindset and lifestyle. We must live *on purpose*. Just as we began our communication with God exactly where we were, we need to start making lifestyle choices at that same point.

We are never going to win a battle we refuse to fight. I'm going to touch on five areas of intentional living that were essential for me. 1. Hygiene and Appearance 2. Spinal Health 3. Exercise 4. Nutrition 5. Laughter. Depending on where you are in your journey will determine how you prioritize them.

1. **Hygiene and Appearance**.

Sometimes getting out of bed can be a monumental task. It feels great to stay in bed to escape reality when a wound is fresh and raw. We have discussed earlier how the enemy would bombard my thoughts as I was waking. My first choice was to dig back down into the covers and refuse the day.

The best thing to do when waking up to a mental battle is to shower. That sounds simple but it gives you a foothold on the day. Water is so revitalizing. We discussed earlier in this book how our tears cleanse our soul. The water in the shower tends to cleanse the depressing thoughts we wake up with. The warm water will also relax muscles and release tension. A shower just simply makes us feel better.

Don't only shower, dress up. Speaking to the girls here: Even if you are wearing jeans that day, do your hair, put make up on, put on a couple pieces of jewelry, and be the best YOU, you can be. It WILL make a difference in your

RISE

thoughts throughout the day. No matter how you feel: Get Up, Dress Up, Show Up and Never Give Up!!!!!

A couple of years after I moved to Kentucky, I worked primarily from home. There was an obvious difference in the days I got up and got dressed as if I was going to the office. I was more focused and more productive on those days. If I decided to lounge around like I could go back to bed at any minute, I was about half as productive. Intentionally getting up and facing the day is like slapping the enemy in the face. Give it ALL you've got!

You should also treat your body in such a way that it fights for you and not against you. I am going to share with you what works for me in the next three points. If you are under a doctor's care for anything, please seek council before making any major changes in your lifestyle.

2. **Spinal Health**

There is a lot of discussion that goes on about caring for your spine. For me, having regular adjustments on my spine keeps my entire body healthy. When my body is healthy it is working for me and not fighting against me. God made our bodies in such a way that they are designed to heal themselves. They can only do that if we treat them the way He intended.

There's tons of information available on the internet. A person will become confused if they read opinion after opinion. I am no Doctor so I am going to refer to a man I have great respect for and have patterned my health choices after: Dr. Ben Lerner. Dr. Ben has authored nine books including *Body By God* and *One Minute Wellness*, both New York Times, USA Today, and Wall Street Journal best sellers. Dr. Ben was also an All- American wrestler. He was the physician for US Wrestling Team participating in six World Team Competitions and two Olympiads. I chose him because I was personally trained through his workshops and know the information he presents is accurate and brings lasting results. Dr. Ben has an eye- opening training

213

called *Body By God*. I believe every person wanting to obey God by treating their body like a temple should have this information.

As a Doctor of Chiropractic, Dr. Ben Lerner says this about Spinal Health.

"While the body can go weeks without food, days without water and a few minutes without air, it cannot survive for a second without nerve (brain) supply. This is because the nerve supply is the literal life and power supply.

The brain and immune system talk to each other and this process is essential for maintaining homeostasis (the balance of health).

By finding a Doctor of Chiropractic who is trained in the full correction and stabilization of the spine and nervous system, you not only remove pain you restore:

- The full communication between the brain and immune system
- Full function of the sympathetic nervous system, which plays a role in controlling every part of the body.
- Immune organ activity, which includes maximum function of the lymph nodes, thymus, spleen, tonsils, bone marrow and associated tissues.

The spine is the lifeline of the entire body. Certain chiropractors are trained to restore normal alignment and proper curvature to the whole spinal column. Seek a Doctor of Chiropractic who is capable of X-raying your spine and determining what it would take to create maximum correction."[1]

I personally discovered the importance of spinal health care when I was in my twenties. I was in a sledding accident which caused damage to my neck. Overtime, I began to develop migraine headaches. I was instructed to see a chiropractor. The migraine would almost instantly disappear after the adjustment. I noticed too, when I got my neck adjusted that my sinuses would clear up. Once I received the education on how the nerves to our face travel through our spine, it made perfect sense why my sinuses cleared up when the C-2 was adjusted.

Through a marketing job I met someone with an amazing story about spinal health that was near and dear to my heart. He was also a Chiropractor. There were complications when his daughter was born. She was laid to the side for dead. As he looked at her laying on the table, the emotional father kicked out and the doctor kicked in. He turned the tiny infant and began spinal adjustments. By aligning the spine immediately after birth, it brought life to that little body. As of the writing of this book his daughter is a teenager.

Again, I am sharing what has worked for me continually for years and stories I personally know to be true. I believe my ability to fight off the depression I battled was primarily because my body was fighting for me and not against me. Have you ever seen a garden hose with a kink in it? Did you notice how the water could not get through? It is the same with the nerves going through our spine. When the spine is out of line is it like kinking the flow of information from our brain to our body. Our body depends on that flow to function properly.

3. **Exercise**

Whether it is a walk around the block or a strenuous goal oriented program, there is no denying that exercise makes us feel better.

Over the years, I have gone from playing competitive tennis to hit and miss with exercising. I can feel the mental difference when my body gets sluggish. I'm sure most of the women reading this can quote the cycle with me: Begin exercising, doing great, exercising regularly, stress hits, skip exercise, crave comfort foods filled with starch and sugar, clothes get tighter, need new clothes, depression deepens while trying on new clothes, begin feeling sluggish and moving slower, avoid mirrors, recognize need to start the cycle again.

My daily walks became my prayer time. Sometimes I would leave the house dragging and feeling defeated. After walking a few miles, getting sunshine and fresh air, and talking to God I felt like an entirely different person.

Let's check in with Dr. Ben to hear his thoughts about exercise:

"Mentally, our brains are programmed to go through a specific sequence of emotional states following emotional trauma or stress. Grieving and mourning are completely natural and necessary states that your brain processes through in order to move past events and work through realities of life. This explains why people that are temporarily relieved of their depression by antidepressant medication eventually end up chronically depressed. Their brain never went through the appropriate process necessary to establish peace with the situation.

Fortunately, there are natural ways to increase your brain's serotonin levels, and curtail your mind into a positive state:

- Exercise regularly – Exercise has been shown to increase the endorphins in your brain that promote happiness and fulfillment.
- Address your pain – Sharing your stress or situation with a trusted friend or trained professional will help give you perspective and allow you to share the burden with someone else who can relate to you and help you cope.
- Eat a healthy diet – Eating a diet rich in vegetable and fruit and omega 3 fats and avoiding sugars and grains will allow your insulin and leptin levels to normalize, resulting in reduced inflammation, promote healthy brain function and decreased depression.

- Do something for someone else – Studies have shown that people who volunteer regularly and/or give generously to others, report a higher sense of purpose and self-value.
- Get plenty of vitamin D – Research has shown that people who don't get adequate amounts of vitamin D are up to 11 times more likely to be depressed. The average person needs 30 minutes of sunlight exposure to 40% of their skin exposed between the hours of 11am and 3pm. Or 5000 IU of a quality vitamin D3 supplement. "[2]

4. **Nutrition**

There are numerous teachings on nutrition from books, downloads, marketing programs, opinionated friends and family to certain doctors that say nutrition doesn't matter. Except for that last one, I'd say we could find elements of truth in all of them. Again, with all the confusion circulating it is difficult to know the truth so most people tend to jump from one program to another with no lasting results.

Consistency is crucial for any result. With most programs, weight loss can be achieved by consistently following any weight loss program. You should ask yourself these questions. *Does the weight come back immediately with any variations? Is the program promoting health in the process?*

Programs begin and programs end. Results come and results go. The only lasting nutritional values come with a lifestyle. God made our bodies and programmed them to function very specifically. When we alter that program by feeding them artificial ingredients our bodies begin to play defense. They begin fighting against us instead of fighting for us.

Again, let's check in with Dr. Ben Lerner about nutrition:

"In this world, committing to doing anything right is difficult. No matter what you do, there will always be challenges and natural temptations that pull you away from doing good. I have found that when I am doing something purely for my own sake, it is significantly more difficult to stay committed than if I am doing it for others.

Because a healthier eating program gives you more energy, greater strength, increased mental awareness, and significantly increases the time you will spend here on the planet, what you put in your mouth affects others. When you consider what you are going to put in your mouth (which most people do not consider at all), remember that if you lead a better, longer life, you can do a tremendous amount more for God and the people you love. Pregnant women always say that they are eating for two. I always say that I am eating for three:

- For me
- For the people around me
- For God

When I remind myself of that, I am far more likely to put the right things in my mouth.[3]

To learn more from Dr. Lerner about specifics on the nutrition God intended visit www.DrBenLerner.com

5. **Laughter**

Laughter is the longest lasting and least expensive medicine. I know when you are in a deep state of depression there seems to be very little to laugh at. Finding humor in situations is also an intentional act. Did you know that something as simple as smiling releases endorphins? Try it. Put your heart into it. Think of something, somewhere, or someone that make you happy. Give it one big smile and hold it for ten seconds.

Again, give your body a chance to fight with you and for you. I know sometimes it seems like a long shot but try your best to look at the lighter side of every situation.

Proverbs 17:22 NLT "A cheerful heart is good medicine, but a broken spirit saps a person's strength."

Never give up!!! We have all drifted along our journey. We have all drifted in our prayer life. We have all drifted in our attempts toward healthy lifestyles. We have all let our attitudes drift and begin to see the negative first. Remember, there is NO condemnation. Condemnation, shame, and guilt are direct hits from our enemy. Therefore, there is no guilt in beginning again. Turn your intentions into specific intentional steps.

## THOUGHTS AND DISCUSSION QUESTIONS

1. ON A SCALE OF 1 TO 10 (ONE = NOT AT ALL; TEN = VERY)
   RATE HOW INTENTIONAL ARE YOU TOWARD LIFE?

   _____

2. RATE EACH AREA INDIVUALLY (1: NOT MUCH – 10: A LOT)
   WHERE DO YOU NEED HELP?

   Hygiene and appearance_____

   Spinal Health _____

   Exercise _____

   Nutrition_____

   Laughter _____

3. WHAT WILL BE YOUR FIRST STEP IN BECOMING MORE
   INTENTIONAL?

   _____

   _____

   _____

   _____

   _____

   _____

   _____

   _____

   _____

   _____

   _____

   _____

   _____

# S

# SCRIPTURE FOR THE MOMENT

There is life in God's Word. By absorbing a Scripture for the moment, it can begin healing you.

We have already discussed how hard it is to focus when you are depressed or in shock from a tragedy. One thing I learned to do in the depth of my depression was to pray the Scriptures back to God. I know that seems a little weird, doesn't it? Surely, he knows what they are. What good would it do me to repeat them as I prayed? Well, I discovered two very good reasons. *1. It puts the Word of God in my mind, thoughts and mouth. 2. God is faithful to HIS word.*

Yes, God is faithful to HIS word. What better way to pray than to pray God's words back to him? There are two Scriptures that give us this assurance when we pray this way. JER 1:12 AMP "Then said the Lord to me, You have seen well, for I am **alert** and **active, watching** over **MY word to perform it.**" And in ISAIAH 55:11 AMP "So shall **MY WORD** be that goes forth out of my mouth: it **shall not** return to me void {without producing any effect, useless}, but **it shall accomplish that which I please and purpose,** and **it shall prosper** in the thing for which **I sent** it." Let's look at this last verse in The Message for a little more clarity. "So will the **words** that come out of **MY MOUTH** not come back empty -handed. **They'll do** the work I sent them to do, **they'll complete the assignment I gave them.**"

Wow! That's powerful!! But, where do we start? How do we know what words to pray? I admit, it is easy to get confused and overwhelmed when beginning to read the Bible. Oftentimes, I even get asked which version is best to read. Even though there are many opinions floating around and many religious legalistic judgements when a person doesn't read or quote from a certain one, there is a very simple answer to this question. Read the one that you can understand!!!

I have quoted a lot from THE MESSAGE simply because my book is more of a self- help book than theological debate. I am aware that the KING JAMES version is closest to the original manuscript and THE MESSAGE is a paraphrase. It is important to compare versions for clarity and understanding.

I'll let you in on a cool way to study the Bible. With the technology that is available, at the printing of this book, it is no longer expensive to buy version after version to compare. Simply download the YOU VERSION app on your phone. Inside the app, you have the option to simply click from translation to translation to compare verses and get a clear understanding of their meaning. It is extremely beneficial to do that. You will quickly discover which one is the easiest for you to understand.

We can take this back to Relationship vs Religion. *Religion* makes legalistic rules about reading so much each day, or completing so much reading in a time frame. (There is nothing at all wrong spending a lot of time reading the Bible. I am speaking primarily here to people who are recovering from deep hurt and feel trapped). *Relationship* is more concerned that you can understand and apply what you are reading. God isn't as impressed with our rituals or legalistic way we approach reading His word as He is in us letting those words sink in and transform our lives. He would much rather us take a sentence or two that applies to our situation and dwell on it and let it do its work than to pat ourselves on the back because we met a goal of reading a certain amount of Scripture in a certain amount of time.

I know, it is extremely hard to even think about picking up a Bible or reading Scriptures (much less repeating them) when you are depressed or coming out of the numbness that shock brings. Don't try to swallow a lot of Scripture at one time. As with anything, you could get choked. Simply find a verse that applies to the way you are feeling, the emotion that is holding you down, or the situation you are dealing with that day. Think on that Scripture and pray it back to God throughout the day. When you feel stronger, begin reading all around that verse. See how it fits into the context of the chapter it came from.

I'll help get you started with some of the ones that were significant to me. There are numerous books available that have Scriptures categorized by topics. The one that has been my go to on a regular basis is *The Secret Power of Speaking God's Word* by Joyce Meyer. I have given that book to numerous people over the years to help them quickly and easily find a verse to hold on to. No Scripture book is a replacement for your Bible. They are aids. It is a good way to begin reading your Bible. Pick a Scripture that applies. Repeat it throughout the day. Let it build your faith and begin to change your thoughts.

Remember the enemy wants to bombard you with lies. He will run from the truth because he is nothing but a liar. Let God's Word do your fighting for you. Repeat them out loud a few times if you can. Rest assured He is listening. He even goes so far as to tell us He builds a hedge around us when we pray. PSALM 34:7 "God's angel sets a circle of protection around us while we pray." I believe this is one of the meanings of ZECHARIAH 4:6 NKJV "Not by might, nor by power, but by My Spirit." All we need to do is let the words come out of our mouth and he has an army of angels fighting for us on our behalf. That is amazing love.

I am going to use the thoughts I mentioned earlier in this book that bombarded me as I would try to wake up. I will match Scripture to them. Some are reworded as confessions to be personal.

*"There is no reason to get up....* Deuteronomy 31:8 AMP "The Lord goes before me; He will {march} with me; He will not fail me or let me go or forsake me; I will fear not, neither become broken {in spirit --- depressed, dismayed, and unnerved with alarm}."

*Why should I go on?...* 2 Corinthians 4:8 TLB "When I am pressed down on every side by troubles, I am not crushed and broken. When I am perplexed because I don't know why things happen as they do, I don't give up and quit."

*I am still alone with people all around me....* PSALM 25:16-17 AMP "Turn to me {Lord} and be gracious to me, For I am alone and afflicted. The troubles of my heart are multiplied; Bring me out of my distresses."

*This emptiness inside is going nowhere...*PSALM 34:18 "If my heart is broken, I'll find God right there; if I'm kicked in the gut, He'll help me catch my breath."

*I'd rather sleep than face reality...*ISAIAH 60:1 "I will get out of bed! Wake up. Put my face in the sunlight. God's bright glory has risen for me. The whole earth is wrapped in darkness, all people sunk in deep darkness, But God rises on me, his sunrise glory breaks over me."

*I don't want to eat, thinking of food makes me sick...*PSALM 107:18-19 TLB "They couldn't stand the thought of food, and they were knocking on death's door. 'Lord, help!' they cried in their trouble, and he saved them from their distress."

*I'd go back to sleep but I'd just feel all the heaviness when I woke up again...*ISAIAH 41:13 AMP "The Lord my God holds my right hand; He is the Lord, Who says to me, Fear not; I will help you!"

*If I get up, I'm going to throw up....* EXODUS 23:25 NKJV "I will serve the Lord my God, and he will bless my bread and my water and take sickness away from me"

*Why should I pray? God only puts up with me because he is obligated to...*JEREMIAH 29:11 AMP "For I know the plans and thoughts that I have for you; says the Lord, 'plans for peace and well-being and not for disaster, to give you a future and a hope. Then you will call on Me, and I will hear {your voice} and I will listen to you."

*Do I have enough to survive today?...* PSALM 34:10 TLB "Those who trust in the Lord will lack no good thing."

*I can't sleep but I can't focus either....*2 THESSALONIANS 3:16 AMP "Now may the Lord of peace Himself grant you His peace at all times and in every way {that peace and spiritual well-being that comes to those who walk with him, regardless of life's circumstances]. The Lord be with you all"

You do not have to be in the pit of distress to apply Scriptures. There are answers and expressions for every thought and situation you could ever deal with. The important fact to remember is God is faithful to HIS word that has already been written. You cannot make a deal or bargain with God to change the rules. He has already written the script. (Thus, the word *Scripture*) The Scriptures He has given is the script He has written for the story of our lives. If we follow and stay on script, the story he has planned can be played out. He is not open to rewriting.

Another way to find relevant Scripture is to simply google. For example, if you wanted a something about joy. Type in 'Scripture Joy' and search. That will give you several options. You can usually choose Biblehub.com and it will automatically give you several versions of that verse along with commentary.

Communication with God is so easy. He accepts you right where you are, in all your mess. His desire is that we just talk to Him. If we aren't comfortable doing that, He gives us the words to say that will bring transforming power.

As you begin your journey digging in God's Word you will find hope, clarity, peace, instruction, directions and understanding. You will learn to love certain verses that bring you light and life and you will enjoy discovering verses you never knew were there. Most important, you will realize just how much God loves you, He is FOR you not AGAINST you and what a relationship with Him is truly like.

THOUGHTS AND DISCUSSION QUESTIONS

1. LIST FIVE EMOTIONS, THOUGHTS OR SITUATIONS
   THAT HOLD YOU DOWN.

   _____

   _____

   _____

   _____

   _____

   _____

2. WHAT BOOK OR DEVICES DO YOU HAVE AVAILABLE
   TO YOU FOR SEARCHING SCRIPTURES?

   _____

   _____

   _____

   _____

   _____

   _____

3. FIND YOUR SCRIPTURE FOR THE MOMENT FOR EACH
   ITEM LISTED IN #1.

   _____

   _____

   _____

   _____

   _____

   _____

   _____

   _____

   _____

# E

## ETERNITY

WHY? WHY? WHY? WHY? WHY? WHY? WHY?
There are so many questions that circle around loss.
The pain, heartaches, disappointments and death we
face on this earth leave us desperately seeking. We spend time in
therapy sessions, spiritual counseling and read books after books
looking for answers. We may find some level of acceptance of the
pain but we will never fully understand it.

Without those answers, we naturally feel the need to blame
someone. Most commonly, we ultimately, yet unconsciously, blame
God or at the very least question Him. In our eyes, He seems to
be the only one who could have prevented the pain. Why did He
let something happen? Why didn't He heal?

One of the problems with our view of God as a healer is our
view of death as an end. We see death as failure or punishment on
God's part. God does heal, here and there. On earth or ultimately
in Heaven. Who are we to say because we didn't see the healing
on earth that God doesn't heal? Our reality of Heaven and eternity
needs to be clearer and bigger.

> The bible helps us with this in 1 Corinthians 13 NLT, "Now we
> see things imperfectly, like puzzling reflections in a mirror, but
> then we will see everything with perfect clarity. All that I know
> is partial and incomplete, but then I will know everything com-
> pletely, just as God now knows me completely."

As I was thinking and preparing to write this section, I asked God why is it we have so many unanswered questions concerning our pain? Why do the answers we try to reason never truly satisfy? How can I explain eternity to someone when the reality of it is only in my heart?

His answer was quiet, comforting and direct. *It's not up to you to prove it!!!* God will reveal eternity to anyone seeking to understand it more. You see, we were made in the image of God. He has placed eternity in our hearts!!! We were never originally designed or created to experience death. It was never part of the plan. Earth was created perfect. Humans were created perfect. Man's rebellion brought death, heartache and struggles into the picture. That is why no matter how desperately we seek for answers concerning pain nothing will completely comfort us. We were not made to understand it. We were made to experience eternity and to live forever.

Trying to understand heartache is the point where many people turn to vices. Excesses are most always an expression of unanswered questions concerning pain. Drugs, alcohol, sex, workaholic, and the list goes on. As Christians, we need to do less judging of a person's outward actions and be more concerned with what they are covering up.

With the seed of eternity planted deeply in our hearts, God takes delight in watering it and feeding it. This is when He gives our faith an opportunity to grow. Our faith will give us more strength and courage than our understanding ever could.

The battle in my mind when Daddy passed is a perfect example of this. If you remember, I was struggling believing that Stefan was in Heaven with Jesus. If that were true, how would my Daddy react when he met him, because I had no doubt Daddy was going to Heaven. That was weighing heavily on me. I had spent my entire life pleasing and performing for Daddy while enjoying one of the most open fun relationships a daughter could have with her father. Would I have to live out every single day on earth thinking when he met Stefan his disappointment in me would be greater than the love we had shared? God was so willing to give me what I needed to understand that it was all okay. I got a small glimpse into eternity standing at that hospital window. If only for a second, I saw Daddy and Stefan holding hands and smiling at me. The seed of eternity that is in my heart was watered and it put an end to the mental torment I thought I was going to live with.

Only when we begin embracing eternity, and quit asking questions, do we leave an open door for God to show up. Over the years as I have shared seeing Daddy and Stefan, I've heard other stories proving my little glimpse into eternity was not that rare. Just recently, I learned of the story of a dear precious friend of mine who also got a glimpse of eternity.

Jennifer was gracious enough to share her story with us to build your eternal faith. "My daughter is seeing Heaven before me. She was welcomed into Jesus' arms on Feb 14, 1993. She was all mine for the six months I carried her. How do I know she's in Heaven? When she passed, I was not told of her gender...only that my baby was unrecognizable. Being discharged from the hospital with too many unanswered questions, I went home to 'heal'. However, in my distress, I asked the Lord to let me see my child at least once. I also requested that He allow my child to learn from Ruth of the Old Testament. A few weeks later He granted my wish in a dream.

I dreamed I was walking in a grassy field, drawn to some activity under a weepy big willow tree (which happens to be my favorite tree). Beneath the tree is Ruth and my child. Next to them, rested a beautiful peacock (my favorite animal). Ruth was teaching my child about the Lord and how to sing praises. It was evident my child was a girl because of her long brown hair and ruffled dress! Ruth looked at me and smiled.

After waking from the dream, I was confident that my daughter, Terri Ann, was in the very best hands, in the very best place that God could have provided."

There is not a more tender feeling in a mothers' heart than knowing her child is safe. If you have a child living in Heaven, you can rest assured your child is content, happy, healthy, and perfectly safe.

Did you ever think about the fact that God created us to dream? All you need to do is spend time with a small child. Their ideas and imaginations are constantly running wild. I can't help but believe that is part of what Jesus meant when He told us to come to Him as little children... **come dreaming**!! We are encouraged over and over to dream and think about eternity.

When I think about eternity I think about my family who now live in Heaven. I am not talking about the ones I knew on this earth that have gone before me. I am talking about the ones I never knew.

As I only look at the generation before me, my generation and the generation after me it's a new world I never experienced. Yet, it is just as real, if not more so, than my world I live on earth.

*The generation before me*: My grandmother had four baby girls and one baby boy that were still born. So, I have four aunts and one uncle I never knew.

*My generation*: My mom miscarried a baby before me and possibly one after me. So, I have at least one sibling and possibly two that I have never met. In addition, I frequently visit the grave of a cousin named David who did not live after he was born. Mom has shared with me that some of her sisters and sister in laws also had miscarriages. So, there are several cousins from them, I have never met.

*The generation after me*: Of course, my three babies are waiting for me. I have cousins here on earth who have been grieved with miscarriages and abortions. So, their children are also waiting.

Within just these three generations (only from my mothers' side of the family) there are eleven people, that I know their names, living in Heaven that never experienced any earth time. Plus, the numerous little family members from the miscarriages and abortions that I will learn their names when I meet them.

So, the dream that frequently plays in my mind is of a large green meadow. I see table clothes laying on the ground in different places with yummy food. (no baskets, just pure fresh food). In the background are children laughing and playing and running. The adults caring for them are also involved in the children's activities. I see my sibling(s) playing with my children and all the aunts, uncles and cousins in the background.

Now to make eternity even more real, add to that picture, my Daddy, Randall, my grandparents, cousins, aunts, uncles and friends that I spent earth time with that are no longer here. It is no wonder the Bible tells us we see dimly now but then we will see clearly. The world of eternity is complete and earth, at its' best, is broken.

We were created for eternity and to live forever. Our hearts truly long for a place called home where we have never been.

Today, as you finish reading this book, maybe you also have children living in Heaven (and possibly even playing with mine from time to time). I long for you to know that your child is not dead. Your baby is living, healthy, happy, active and in the very best of care. Because God put eternity in our hearts, He also made a way for us to experience it. He knew from the beginning of time just how broken and heart wrenching this earth would turn out to be. He sent His Son, who was pure, holy and perfect, to this earth to offer us a way to eternity and to be our gate. If we accept the offer of His Son, we too can join Him and hold our babies in Heaven.

That offer has nothing at all to do with church activities or organized religion. It is very simple: We have become part of this broken earth. And because of that, we can never fit into Heaven with our pure little ones without some help. God made it very easy. (Man, on the other hand, has over complicated it and caused much confusion). His Son Jesus, even though He lived on this earth, remained as pure as Heaven. If we simply admit we are broken and He is perfect and He is our only gate to regain the purity to enter Heaven, we indeed can live the everlasting eternity with our babies.

This is the simple- truth behind a verse that is so often treated with such little respect. I am sure you have seen John 3:16 plastered in numerous places. I am not ending this book by plastering it on the pages for you to figure it out. With the deepest sincerity in my heart, I want you to know, if you have a little one you feel was yanked from you here on earth, there is only one way you can hold your baby again. His name is Jesus. John 3:16, 17 NJKV "For God so loved the world that He gave His only begotten Son, that whoever believes in Him should not perish but have everlasting life. For God did not send His Son into the world to condemn the world, but that the world through Him might be saved"

One of the reasons, I even hesitated to quote John 3:16 here, is because John 3:17 is rarely quoted with it. I personally think one should never be quoted without the other. YES, I believe God sent His son to save us. I also believe he DID NOT send Him to condemn and He never intended people who call themselves "Christians" to condemn either.

So, as I mentioned at the beginning of this book I do not intend to "evangelize." I am simply sharing with you what I have learned through the struggles, tragedies and heartaches I have endured. As seen in John 3:16 & 17, if you believe the Bible, God offered a way but is not forcing anyone to take it. I am not a Bible thumper, scream in your face type of person. I just know the heartache of empty arms and want to share the hope I have. If you have questions or want the assurance you can see you baby again, reach out to me at my website. www.Debralynnhayes.com

You see, I cannot prove eternity. It is something in my heart. But I believe with all my heart it is real. You certainly are entitled to your own beliefs. You may say, "You are basing all you have written on the Bible and I'm not even sure I believe anything in the Bible or not so sure about God either." It is perfectly fine to have those thoughts. Even though I was raised in church, when my world fell apart, my beliefs were shaken to the core and I questioned everything I had ever been taught. I can tell you little by little the ideals of religion were destroyed and God proved himself real to me. He will do the same for you.

You may ask, "What if you are wrong?" My answer would be, "What if I am right?" I would much rather live my life with the hope of Heaven and Eternity and find out when it is over that I was wrong than to live each day denying, doubting, or refusing to believe it all and learn when earth time is over that it is true and I missed it.

That is why it is *faith*. Life is hard. Faith is not easy to live. But, we were all put on this earth to help and encourage each other along the way. You can make it. You will survive. Get your glimpse into eternity. Look up and RISE!!!!!

THOUGHTS AND DISCUSSION QUESTIONS:

1. WHAT ARE YOUR CURRENT THOUGHTS ABOUT ETERNITY?

   _____

   _____

   _____

   _____

   _____

   _____

2. LOOK AT THIS PICTURE AND LIST THE FIRST TWELVE THOUGHTS THAT COME TO MIND.
   (ex. Freedom, play, unrestricted, doing flips in the air)
   Do you see fear or freedom?

_____
_____
_____
_____

3. ASK GOD FOR YOUR GLIMPSE INTO ETERNITY AND
   DESCRIBE THE PICTURE IN YOUR MIND.

_____
_____
_____
_____
_____
_____
_____
_____
_____
_____
_____
_____
_____
_____
_____
_____
_____
_____
_____
_____
_____
_____

# END NOTES

Authors Note
1. "Breathe. (2AM)" – Anna Nalick -American singer songwriter

Introduction
1. WHAC A MOLE™ - Federal Registered Trademark by Mattel, Inc. serial number 86264359

Part One KNOCKED DOWN
1. "Undefeated" Collin Raye used by permission

Chapter 1 A BEAUTIFUL BEGINNING—A THREAD OF LONELINESS
1. "American Pie" – 1971 song by American folk rock singer and song writer Don McLean.
2. "Flight of the Bumblebee" - is an orchestral interlude written by Nikolai Rimsky-Korsakov for his opera The Tale of Tsar Saltan, composed in 1899–1900.
3. "Wichita Lineman" - is a song written by American songwriter Jimmy Webb in 1968. It was first recorded by American country music artist Glen Campbell
4. "Flight of the Bumblebee"
5. "Fur Elise" - Bagatelle No. 25 in A minor for solo piano, commonly known as "Für Elise" or "Fuer Elise", is one of Ludwig van Beethoven's most popular compositions.
6. Wichita Lineman"

## Chapter 4 WAS UNLIKE HIM TO BE LATE—THEN THE PHONE CALL CAME

1. Kary Oberbrunner, *The Deeper Path* (Grand Rapids, MI: Baker Books, 2013)

## Part Two CRAWLING

1. "Undefeated" Collin Raye used by permission

## Chapter 26 FREEBIRD—BUT NOT THE TWENTY MINUTE VERSION

1. "Freebird" is a power ballad performed by American rock band Lynyrd Skynyrd. The song was first featured on the band's debut album in 1973.
2. IBID
3. IBID
4. "Angel" (**Sarah McLachlan song**) "**Angel**" Single **by Sarah McLachlan**; from the album Surfacing and City of Angels; Released: November 24, 1998
5. IBID
6. "Amazing Grace" is a Christian hymn published in 1779, with words written by the English poet and Anglican clergyman John Newton.
7. IBID
8. "STAR TREK II: The Wrath of Khan" (Paramount Pictures, 1982)

## Chapter 34 LIFE CAME FAST—AND WENT FULL CIRCLE

1. Kary Oberbrunner, *The Deeper Path* (Grand Rapids, MI: Baker Books, 2013)

## Part Three SITTING

1. "Undefeated" Collin Raye used by permission

## Chapter 35 SITTING—NECESSARY, BUT HAZARDOUS

1. Washington Post Jan 20, 2014.

## Chapter 37 I TRADED A WEEKEND WITH KEVIN COSTNER—FOR THIS

1. "TIN CUP" is a 1996 romantic comedy film co-written and directed by Ron Shelton, and starring Kevin Costner and Rene Russo with Cheech Marin and Don Johnson.

## Chapter 40 DEAD-END DISTRACTIONS...............TIME TO ELIMINATE

1. Kary Oberbrunner, *The Deeper Path* (Grand Rapids, MI: Baker Books, 2013)

## Chapter 43 SOMETIME SALVATION—IS IN THE EYE OF THE STORM

1. "Sometimes Salvation" The Black Crowes were an American rock band formed in 1989. ... some members of the band did reunite to play "Sometimes Salvation" with Gov't Mule

## Chapter 50 FIND YOUR DIRT—AND YOU WILL GROW

1. "The Passion Of The Christ" (also known simply as The Passion) is a 2004 American biblical epic drama film directed by Mel Gibson, written by Gibson and Benedict Fitzgerald, and starring Jim Caviezel as Jesus Christ.
2. "Hero" is the first single of the 2009 album Awake by the Christian rock band Skillet and is the first track on the album.

## Part Four RISE

1. "Undefeated" Collin Raye used by permission

## R RELATIONSHIP...........NOT RELIGION

1. Faye Brown Stiles, licensed minister, West Tennessee Grace Network (Daily Bible Snippets on Facebook) used by permission

## I INTENTIONAL LIVING

1. Dr. Ben Lerner used by permission
2. IBID
3. IBID

# ACKNOWLEDGEMENTS

To Jesus – You are indeed the author of my story and the finisher of my faith.

To My Parents- for raising me with a foundation of love. Thank-you Daddy, for teaching me to laugh and always find the lighter side of life. Thank- you Mama, for your continual support and unconditional love.

My Bunko Babes – Your encouragement, belief and excitement early in this project will never be forgotten.

Cindy – What a tireless and faithful friend!! Thank you for your support not only as I lived through the pages of this book but also reliving them with me as I wrote it.

Collin Raye, Thank-you for contributing so quickly to this project at a critical time when I needed the inspiration to move forward. You understand what it is like to put a heartache on paper. (one of America's best-loved country singers. www.collinraye.com)

Connie – Thank you for always having my back. (You be Thelma, I be Louise)

Craaybeek Family – Even though we are currently spread out in every direction of this country, every single one of you will always be family in my heart.

Deana – Where would my life be today without your forwarded post? Thank You!!!!

Dr. Ben Lerner – Thank you for teaching me how to let my body naturally fight for me instead of against me. Your contribution to this book brings tremendous value. www.DrBenLerner.com

Erik – My truth teller! Thank you for speaking truth into my fears.

Equus Run Vineyards – Such a beautiful haven. Thank you for providing many peaceful afternoons of writing. www.equusrun-vineyards.com

Gary and Tracy – There are no more words!!!!! Love you two BIG!!!!

Igniting Souls Tribe – Your friendship and support is amazing. I am blessed to travel this journey with each of you. I continue to be inspired daily as I see God use your lives to impact others for Him.

Jennifer – Thank you for sharing such a tender place in your heart. I bet our little ones play together daily.

Jill – Thank for being you being constant through my emotional ups and downs of writing and for offering Double J Ranch to me as a haven, escape and second home. Love you.

Kary – Thank you for turning "I Believe In You" to "I'll Show You How." This book would never have become a reality without your coaching and insight.

Laura – My new old friend. Your consulting has made me a better writer. Thank you for not just editing the book but for teaching me in the process.

La Z Boy Friends – The ones who truly saw what daily tolls writing took on me as I emotionally revisited the events in this book. Thank you for your understanding.

Linda – My spiritual cheerleader!!! Love ya girl!!!

Lucas – You have always followed the Truth! You have a special place in my heart as well as Gods'. He has BIG plans for you.

Mark and Debbie – Mark, thank you for the many years of friendship and for always being my safe place to take off my mask before I was ready to keep it off. Debbie – Thank you for sisterhood and sharing your husband with so many for the sake of the Kingdom.

Pastor Pat and Jackie – Your love, support and wisdom was exactly what I needed to keep focused on God when I wanted to run. It was no accident that God moved us to your ministry in Ohio at the time he did.

Rick, Bettina and Ms. Bette – Thank you for making Mom and I part of your family. You are a blessing beyond words.

Sissy n Law – (whom I did not divorce) Thank you for being the sister I never had as we shared many tears and good times. You will always be the best aunt ever. I look forward to spending eternity with you and all your nephews.

The Ex – I deeply appreciate the time you spent editing through each word in this story to assure accuracy and for giving your blessing to share our lives, our children and our mistakes with the world.

Turner Family – Thank you for believing in me and including me in *Maggie's Light* long before *RISE* was finished.

Victory Life Church – My beautiful bouquet of wildflowers. A bunch of imperfect people who love the Lord and love each other. I thank God daily for planting me with you.

There is an incredible group of people who went over and beyond to help make this book a reality. The financial outlay to begin the process was a large mountain staring me in the face. These people stepped up and planted financial seeds into this project. Words are not adequate to express the gratitude in my heart.

Steve and Pam Ball, Mike and Kathy Flynn, Quentin Seals, Jeff, Tesha, Lucas and Matthew Hinkle, Martha Gulley, Rick and Bettina Sharp, Vickie Woods, Deana Fleming, Chris Reddick, Linda Hudson, Gary and Tracy Toney, Bob Smiddy, Mark and Debbie Williams, Angela Dee, Kent and Andrea Metcalf, Ramon Rodriquez, Vaughn and Lillie Turner, Greg and Connie Sexton, Jan Denman, Janet Dalton, Faye Stiles, Donna Knight Horner, Tim and Amy Turner, Janet Purkey, Theresa Shepard, Traci Webb, Cathy Scott, Lori Carmichael, Bobby and Diane Cupp, Cynthia Akins, Kathleen Roy, Jim and Cindy Amburn, Laura Gill, Jared Smith, Kaye McGuffin Schwalb, Christina Fannin, Alice Westmoreland, Lisa Phelps, Karen Rolfes, Amber Reagan, Susan Bartley, Nancy Bible, Joe Fields, Jim and Char McCurn, My late aunt Marie Darden

# ABOUT THE AUTHOR

**Debra Lynn Hayes** has a passion to encourage others to overcome loss and tragedy. As a former corporate trainer and liaison of an international company, she strategized success with individuals and teams. Today as an author, speaker and coach she focuses those same skills to empower others facing personal devastation. For years, she lived behind her own mask and knows what it takes to remove it.

Debra is a certified trainer, coach and speaker for:

*Your Secret Name* ™ A guided journey to discover your true- identity. We all have the limitation of our birth names and the damaging effects of given names. We can never outlive our own self- image. Reset your self-image and discover who you were created to be.

*The Deeper Path* ™ Do you feel like you've lost your way? Maybe you've just lost your why. To go higher you must first go deeper. Get a GPS for your dreams. In the Deeper Path Coaching Cohort you'll craft your working or playing. (To yourself it will appear like you're be doing both.) By facing your deepest pain, you often discover your greatest potential.

*The Road to RISE* ™: Have you experienced a disappointment or tragedy that has seemed to define your life? Do you feel stuck? Discover the steps to lead you back on a path to contentment. The Road to Rise will guide you as you navigate through pain and begin dreaming again.

To contact Debra for speaking or
coaching opportunities:

**EMAIL**
**Debralynnhayesauthor@gmail.com**

**WEBSITE**
**Debralynnhayes.com**

**FACEBOOK**
**Debralynnhayes**

If *RISE* has had an impact on you,
Debra would love to hear from you.